PRIMARY
PRINTS

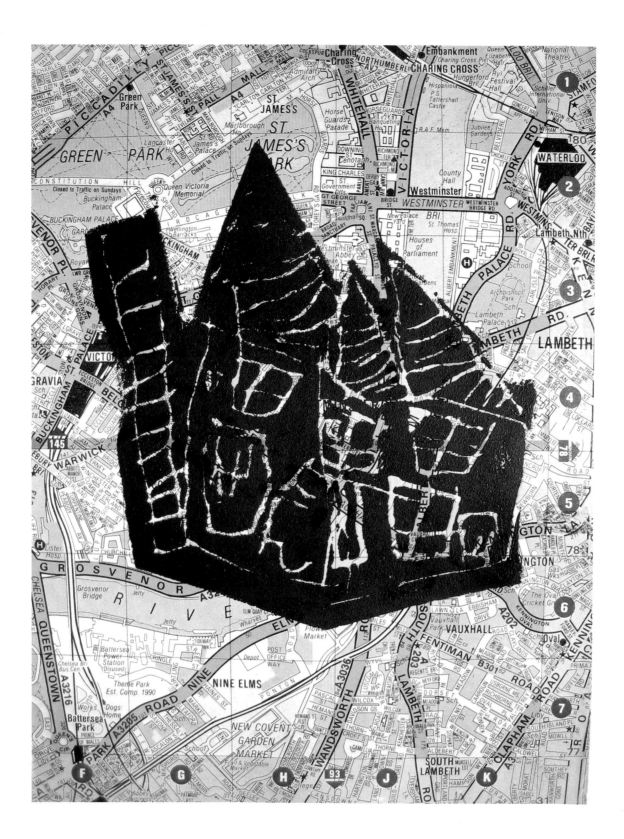

PRIMARY PRINTS

Creative printmaking
in the classroom

Anne Desmet

A&C Black • London

First published in Great Britain in 2010
A&C Black Publishers Limited
36 Soho Square
London W1D 3QY
www.acblack.com

ISBN: 978-14081-1143-7

CIP Catalogue records for this book are available from the British Library and the U.S. Library of Congress.

Typeset in 11 on 13pt Minion

Book design by Susan McIntyre
Cover design by Sutchinda Thompson
Commissioning editor: Susan James

Printed in China by C&C offset Printing.

A&C Black uses paper produced with elemental chlorine-free pulp, harvested from managed sustainable forests.

Safety note: Every effort has been made to ensure that all of the information in this book is accurate. Due to differing conditions, tools, materials and individual skills neither the publishers nor the author can be held responsible for any injuries, losses and other damages that may result from the use of information in this book. Children should be closely supervised while working on these projects, and you should always follow manufacturers' instructions and safety guidelines when working with various tools and materials. Always store inks and chemicals (clearly labelled) out of the reach of children.

Half title page: *My house* by Reception Class child. Polystyrene block printed in black ink on London A-Z map page

Frontispiece: *My house* by Reception Class child. Polystyrene block print in black ink on London map page

Title page: *Hybrid building* by Year 5 child. Linocut and stencil print in white and red inks on khaki Canford paper

Contents page: Stencil print by Reception Class child, in red and black inks on white paper

Contents

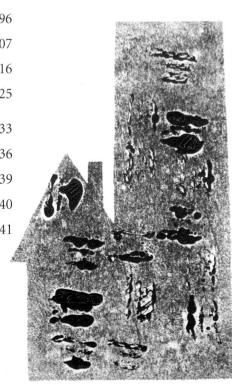

*For Marion, Thomas and all the children of Lauriston School,
past, present and future*

Flying a kite on Parliament Hill by Year 3 child. Collagraph and stencil print in cream, red and black inks on blue-green Nepalese Lhokta paper

LEFT *London bus with St Paul's and the London Eye* by Year 2 child. Two-plate cereal box collage print on white Somerset Satin paper. The first plate was printed with a purple/lilac ink blend; the second was printed in black. Photo © Madeleine Waller 2008

Acknowledgements

I am indebted to Peter Sanders, Deputy Headteacher at Lauriston School, Hackney, for inviting me to undertake the ambitious printmaking project that inspired this book. Thanks are also due to Creative Partnerships, East London, for funding the project; my children – Thomas and Marion – for testing out my print ideas at home; my husband, Roy Willingham, for his unfailing quiet support; Intaglio Printmaker Ltd and Paintworks Ltd (both of London) for all the art materials used; the staff at Lauriston School for their enthusiastic support and for their photographs of the children printing; Madeleine Waller for photographing the children's artworks and turning them into digital books; to Francis Marshall and colleagues at the Museum of London and to the Guanlan Print Industry Base, Shenzhen, China, both of which museums acquired the artists' books that directly inspired this book; David Morris of the Whitworth Art Gallery for advice on print collections; Phil Alden for proofreading; Linda Lambert and Susan James of A&C Black Publishers, for their ongoing support over many years; and finally, a huge thank you to the children of Lauriston School who made prints with me. It was a real pleasure to work with you. You far exceeded my high expectations and without your hard work I would never have written this book, which I hope that you and many others will enjoy.

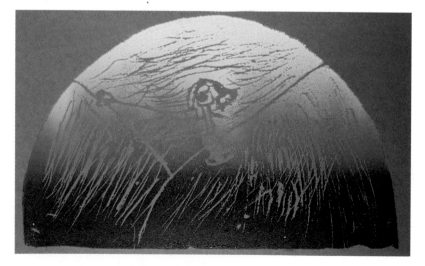

Girl flying a kite by Year 3 child.
Polystyrene block print in a yellow/blue blend on purple Canford paper

Introduction

Printmaking offers a wealth of ways to make richly textured, memorable images, each technique having its own characteristics. Many methods can be carried out on a table at home or in class. They require little specialist equipment and can be undertaken at minimal expense and to great effect by anyone – from highly experienced professional artists, to art students, to school children and their parents who may never have made a print before in their lives.

Printmaking is the art of transferring an image created on one object onto the surface of another, rather than directly drawing or painting it. Methods involving a printing block can produce multiple replicas of the same original image; this led, early in the 20th century, to the concept of the limited edition print. The potential to replicate accurately the same picture also revolutionised the field of pattern-

HSBC bank and Tower of London by Year 5 child. Linocut and stencilling in blue and yellow inks on black Canford paper

9

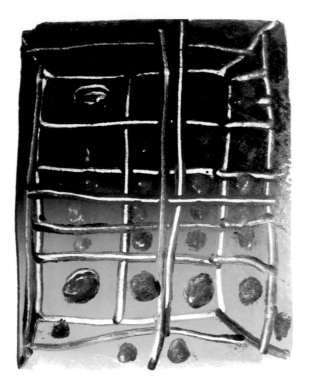

making. The possibilities too of using the same printing plate to produce experimental, non-identical, compositions or colour variants, or of combining different print processes within the same image, are areas that offer endless scope for creativity.

Printmaking offers the potential to make images even more inventive, unusual and surprising than those created directly by paintbrush, pen or pencil. Techniques such as linocutting or polystyrene-block-printing may produce crisp, linear, sharp-edged imagery, whilst an indented Plasticine block or plate made from a cereal-box collage might print with surprisingly textural effects. Many surfaces can be printed including plain or pre-printed papers (such as street maps and gift wrap), card, wallpaper, fabric and acetate; often too, home-made printing blocks make pleasing art objects in their own right.

Sophisticated printed material abounds, from advertising hoardings to chocolate wrappers, yet fine prints can be made using all sorts of everyday materials such as broccoli florets, dried pasta shapes, cardboard boxes and cotton buds. This book describes a range of such low-tech, low-cost methods showing how they can be used singly or together to produce unusual, ambitious, professional results and they can all be undertaken without a printing press – printing simply by hand or using roller pressure.

ABOVE LEFT *Untitled* by Reception class child. Monotype (wiping method – drawn with cotton bud) in a blue/green ink blend on Japanese paper

ABOVE RIGHT *Canary Wharf Tower* by Year 1 child. Polystyrene block print in a blue/green ink blend on mustard-yellow Nepalese Lhokta paper

RIGHT *Canary Wharf Tower* by Year 4 child. Plasticine block print with stencilling, sponge and various DIY printers using green, blue and white inks on red Nepalese Lhokta paper. Photo © Madeleine Waller 2008

Over a decade ago I embarked, with fellow-artist Jim Anderson, on the journey of discovery that led to our book: *Handmade Prints – an introduction to creative printmaking without a press* (published by A&C Black, 2000; reprinted 2003 and 2006). My own specialism within printmaking is the exacting skill of wood engraving and, allied to that, I make linocuts and occasional monotypes (one-off prints – see *Glossary of terms*, p.134). For some 20 years too, as well as creating editioned relief prints, I have made increasingly experimental collages using found materials such as seashells, mirror fragments, broken glass, ceramic tiles and roofing slate as the 'canvas' on which to adhere a variety of my own lino- and woodblock-printed papers. The research Jim and I undertook for *Handmade Prints* diversified my own artistic practice enormously. Its open-minded, playful approach to technique has been a major influence in my own creative thinking and teaching ever since.

When Peter Sanders, Deputy Headteacher of Lauriston School, Hackney (a London primary school known for its commitment to

ABOVE *London skyline with pigeons* by Year 5 child. Linocut and stencil printed in white and yellow inks on maroon Canford paper

RIGHT *Statue and skyline* by Year 3 child. Collagraph (with patterned corrugated card), stencilling, sponge and various DIY printers in green, cream and black inks on red Nepalese Lhokta paper

12

Column tops of portico: St Leonard's Church, Shoreditch by Year 6 child. Linocut printed in a blue/yellow ink blend on khaki Canford paper

the arts), invited me to work with children and staff from every class in the school – from three- to eleven-year-olds – to teach a variety of print techniques and to produce two artists' books, I jumped at the chance. The proposed project seemed to offer the perfect opportunity for me to reconsider and further develop many of the print processes I had investigated for *Handmade Prints* – with the exciting possibility of mixing and layering them to produce rich, multi-media artworks. Over some 20 workshops spanning four months, more than 600 unique and original prints were produced. These ranged from panoramic vistas worked on by entire classes, to a diverse array of small-scale prints by individual children. The quality, range and ambition of the children's work far exceeded my expectations and directly inspired this book.

In the hope of encouraging others, working alone or with groups of all ages, to discover or revisit the delights of printmaking, I have set out the techniques we used, as well as the organisational aspects of working with classes of 30 – from toddlers to pre-teens. Because the specific theme I was working on was: 'Our London', it was designed to involve consideration of London's architecture; thus most of the resulting prints feature buildings or cityscapes. Remember, however, that all techniques described have any number of applications by no means limited to architectural imagery. You can use them to produce prints on any theme under the sun! The more straightforward as well as the elaborate mixed-media prints here will, I hope, simply serve as vehicles to expand the creative horizons of printmaking without a press.

Star Wars by the author's son, Thomas, Year 5. Monotype (drawing method) in black ink on a blue/orange, fibre-textured, Japanese paper. Made at home as a demonstration print for teaching monotype in class

1 *Equipment and materials*

To carry out the techniques described, you will need:

1 Desk or clean table (if working with a class of 30, you will need at least six tables – standard-sized trestle tables are ideal – allowing one for every six children, with a spare for laying out equipment).

2 Inking slab (if working with a class you will need at least six, but for some projects you may need as many as 30 – see specific chapters for details). This might be:

   a A smooth sheet of Perspex® (Plexiglas), vinyl, toughened glass (with smooth edges), metal or marble, ideally at least 305x203mm (12x8in.).

   b A clean, metal baking tray, smooth ceramic tile, Melamine or Formica®-covered kitchen chopping board or uncut lino block.

   c If you don't want to clean slabs after use, make disposable ones from acetate sheets. These cost less than £1 for an A4-sized sheet at art materials shops. Ensure the tabletop you are using is smooth, as acetate will not make a useable slab on a rough surface. Tape the acetate down along all four sides, using masking or clear tape; this will stop it sliding about while you are rolling ink and also, as acetate is so thin, will prevent the sheet wrapping itself around the roller as you ink it. Acetate can also act as a substitute for printing paper, printing with stained-glass-like effects.

   d A large side of an old cereal box* (or similar stiff card or mountboard with one glazed/shiny surface) taped along its edges to a smooth worktable makes another cost-free, disposable, ink slab. Tape it printed-side-up as its shiny surface will withstand ink whereas the unprinted side will absorb it and go soggy. (*Only ink cereal-box slabs with regular oil-based or oil-based water-washable printing ink as water-based will soak into the card whether shiny side up or not.)

   e A4-size (US: A-size), wipe-clean, white boards. Lauriston School happened to have a large stack of these, regularly used in class for writing with wipe-clean markers. These are perfect mini ink slabs especially when children are working on monotypes (for which each child needs their own slab – see Chapter 4) and they can be easily cleaned afterwards.

Dragon in China Town by Year 2 child. Two-plate cereal box card print on white Somerset Satin paper. The background plate was inked in a green/blue blend; the 'dragon' plate was inked in black

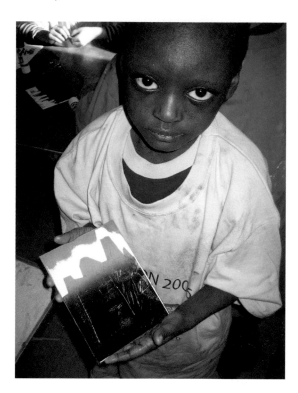

3 Printing ink (see p.19).

4 Printing paper (see p.22). You will also need scrap paper or small sketchbooks plus tracing paper for reversing images and to make paper stencils; it can be bought in A4-size (US: A-size) pads or much larger sizes.

5 Smooth-edged palette knife (available from art materials shops).

6 Reasonably sharp scissors or craft knife (children's use must be supervised).

7 Sticky tape (masking tape, ideally).

8 Pencils, erasers, sharpeners, cheap biro pens.

9 Box of cotton buds (available from any chemist shop/drugstore).

10 Hand-held mirror: imagery, especially writing, must be created back-to-front on a printing block in order to print the right way around. A mirror reflecting the block helps you to see how your image will look when printed.

11 Tub of barrier cream (to protect hands from ink). Alternatively, wear rubber or latex gloves to clean up.

12 Apron(s) (or loose-fitting old T-shirts) to protect clothing.

13 Plastic clothesline or strong cord (and lots of clothes pegs) strung across the workroom for hanging wet prints to dry.

ABOVE LEFT Year 2 child with cereal box card printing plate, still wet with Caligo™ ink after printing with a purple/lilac colour blend. Behind is a table with glue sticks and scissors used in the making of other cereal box printing blocks

ABOVE RIGHT *House and car in China Town* by Year 2 child. Two-plate cereal box collage print on white Somerset Satin paper. The first plate was printed with a purple/lilac ink blend; the second was printed in red

14 Stack of newspapers to protect work surfaces (or tape polythene sheets or garbage bags to tabletops, to keep them clean, and wipe down the polythene between printings or dispose of and replace protective newspaper layer as required).

15 Washing-up liquid, water, household cream cleaner and cooking oil (a light, cheap oil like sunflower is ideal) for cleaning up ink.

16 Bag of clean rags and/or paper towels for cleaning up; baby wipes are useful for instant clean-up of fingers, palette knives, etc., but are an expensive way to tackle the entire clean-up.

17 Plastic washing-up bowl or access to a sink.

18 Plastic rubbish sacks taped to the edges of several worktables for instant disposal (for recycling) of dirty newspapers, duff prints etc.

19 Collection of small man-made and/or natural sponges for printing. (I have had, for years, a children's set of printing sponges. It contains some 20 small sponges of different shapes and has been invaluable when I've been working with school groups over three or four years. The sponges are now falling to bits but I've had lots of use from them. Snap them up from toyshops!)

20 Three or four printing rollers, one of at least 90mm wide x c.38–50mm diameter (c.3.5in. wide x c.1.5–2in. diameter) – and two or three between 150–200mm wide (6–8in.). Inexpensive hard and soft rubber rollers (with wooden or plastic handles) are available from art and craft shops; they perform very well for all techniques

Using a mirror to view an image in reverse as an aid for creating a design on a printing block

17

described. (At far greater cost but excellent performance come brass-framed, polyurethane or Durathene™ rollers – a worthwhile investment if you plan to pursue printmaking professionally.)

21 Make a fabric dabber for adding extra localised colours to a roller-inked block. You will need: an old sock or pair of tights, a rough circle of smooth cotton rag (old shirt or bed sheeting is ideal) of c.20cm (8in.) diameter and a piece of string. Scrunch up sock or tights into a tight ball and place in the centre of the rag, gather up the rag edges around the sock ball and tie the string tightly around the 'neck', like a sack, so that the sock-ball is squashed as hard and compact as possible inside. To use it for inking: hold the 'sack' by its tied-up neck and dab the 'ball' end into the wet ink on the slab, then dab the inked dabber onto selected areas of block.

22 Collection of bits and pieces to use as printers: polystyrene sheets – (such as the circular base-plates in pre-packaged pizzas, or flat sections cut from polystyrene burger boxes); Plasticine; buttons; paper clips; bits of wood; string; pipecleaners; cardboard (corrugated and smooth); bubble wrap; scrunched tin foil; wood or plastic toy bricks; Lego® bricks; dried pasta shapes; broccoli or cauliflower florets sliced in half lengthways (vegetable blocks shrivel with keeping so prepare these the evening before printing); plastic fridge-magnet letters and numbers; old toy cars and trucks with textured tyres (difficult to clean, so don't use any that are precious); scraps of lace or other textured fabrics and so on.

BELOW LEFT Plastic tub of variously textured DIY printing blocks waiting to be cleaned after printing

BELOW Pencil study on white cartridge paper for *City street* polystyrene block print (on facing page)

18

23 First aid kit. Hopefully you won't use this but if you plan to do linocutting with school children, be prepared, with sticking plasters, for stabbed fingers!

INK

There are many different brands of printing ink and each has its own characteristics. It comes in tins, bottles and tubes. I find tubes easiest as ink is less prone to drying between printing sessions (provided you replace caps tightly!) than when stored in tins or bottles. Amongst the 'relief printing inks' (which are what you need to undertake all techniques in this book), there are various types:

Oil-based inks

These print consistently well (and are environmentally-friendly provided they are cleaned up with vegetable oil followed by washing-up liquid, rather than with white spirit) but they cannot be easily cleaned off clothing and other fabrics; so, whilst excellent for adult use, they are probably not suitable in primary schools.

City street by Year 1 child. Polystyrene block print in a green/blue ink blend on mustard-yellow Nepalese Lhokta paper

ABOVE *Hills and 5 Towers* by Year 3 child. Polystyrene block print on olive-green Canford paper, printed in a yellow/red blend of Caligo™ water-washable relief printing ink

LEFT Polystyrene block (section of pizza tray) for *Hills and 5 Towers*, after printing

Water-based inks

Water-based ink, being washable with water, is easy to wash off skin, clothes and work surfaces so is more viable in schools. Some brands become waterproof once dry so, ideally, clean them up while still wet. Washable or not, some colours do stain fabric. Water-based inks tend to dry quickly especially (with brands I tried) reds and whites. Cure this by mixing in, with palette knife, one drop of washing-up liquid with the ink on the slab before rolling and printing.

Papers printed with water-based ink often cockle as the ink dries. To avoid or reduce this, interleave freshly printed papers with kitchen baking parchment (this is usually a silicone-release paper to which damp ink does not adhere) and stack them in a pile with blotting paper at the top and bottom. Weigh the stack down with books and leave to dry for at least a week. It can help to dampen the back of each printed paper by misting it with water from a plant spray before weighing it down.

Among specialist Japanese tissue-like papers, some (such as Shoji) are designed for water-based inks and barely seem to cockle at all. With water-based inks, generally, you get better results if you allow each newly-printed layer to dry before adding fresh layers. If printing wet-on-wet, colours tend to get muddy and paper is more likely to cockle.

Water-washable oil-based inks

This is a relatively recent development: a vegetable-oil-based ink washable with warm soapy water. It combines the excellent printing quality of oil-based inks with a relatively easy clean-up. Colours can be successfully printed wet-on-wet and there is no paper-cockling. The brand I favour is Caligo™ water-washable relief printing ink. It is available from specialist printmaking suppliers and by mail order and comes in tubes or tins in many colours. I used it for all projects in this book. As I was working to a budget, I ordered only black, white and the primaries: red, yellow and blue, so I could mix any other hues as needed. I also ordered tubes of extender – a 'transparent ink' that looks and feels like set honey but which, when added to a colour, renders it more translucent so that, when overprinted onto another colour, a third hue is created where the first and second overlap. The school and I were highly impressed with these inks, their only drawback being that, if hot water was unavailable or ink had dried, they were hard to clean off rollers and slabs. They were, however, much easier to clean off glass than off Perspex® (Plexiglas) or lino slabs and adding some household cream cleaner to the soapy water helped. Stubborn stains can also be cleaned off with liquid soap undiluted with water or with vegetable oil.

Wooden- and plastic-handled rubber rollers, tubes of Caligo™ water-washable relief printing inks, Perspex® (Plexiglas) inking slab and ink rolled in a two-colour blue/yellow blend

PAPER

You will need lots of it. Look for smooth papers rather than heavily textured types.

Cheap and readily-available papers

These all work very well for all techniques described: plain newsprint; printer/photocopier paper; Canford (comes in A4 sheets in a wide range of colours); cartridge; brown; sugar paper; giftwrap (for pattern/texture under your own printing); streetmaps or Ordnance Survey map pages; and wallpaper lining paper. Bear in mind, however, that cheaper papers are usually made from acidic wood pulp, which causes the paper to brown and become brittle with age and/or exposure to sunlight.

Specialist printmaking papers

There are many specialist papers. They are not essential but may help. The same print can look radically different depending on the paper used, so it helps to try out a variety. Here are a few favourites, all of which print well for all techniques described and are fairly widely available from good art materials' suppliers: China White laid; Kozu-shi; Tosa Washi and Shoji (all tissue-like but deceptively strong Japanese papers); handmade coloured papers such as Nepalese Lhokta (surprisingly cheap for large sheet-sizes) in rich, warm colours – the surface texture is inconsistent but printing, especially with sponge printers, is highly effective. With thicker papers, 'burnishing' (printing a block by rubbing with hand or hand-held tool such as a spoon) is harder as there is higher risk of the paper slipping during printing, but roller-printing them is highly effective. Good, heavier-weight papers are Somerset satin (hot pressed, white, British); and Zerkall (off-white, bright white or cream, German).

Good quality papers like these are often made with cotton fibres or purified wood pulp, so are less prone to ageing problems. They vary widely in price and decorative qualities. Any reasonable art materials supplier should advise you. Smooth, pure, 'waterleaf' papers (i.e., papers that have not been coated with a gelatine or glue paste called 'size') work well for relief printing, especially in layered colours, as they readily absorb the ink. In some papers, size is mixed into the paper pulp. This is called *internal sizing* and gives the paper extra strength. Paper may be: *HP* (*hot pressed*), making it very smooth – perfect for relief printing; *rough*, which has a coarse texture better suited to broad brush painting; and *CP* (*cold pressed*) or *Not* – a general-purpose paper with a slight texture.

RIGHT *Untitled tower* by Year 6 child. Linocut printed with blue/yellow blend of Caligo™ water-washable inks on purple Canford paper. Photo © Madeleine Waller 2008

BELOW Pencil sketch by Year 1 child in preparation for printmaking

Inking and printing

Printers can be inked and printed in different ways. For the techniques described, all inking was done by hand using simple rubber rollers with, from time to time, additional selective inking with a home-made fabric dabber/pounce.

INKING UP

Mixing ink

Ink comes in numerous great colours so you can squeeze a colour from the tube and print with it. Alternatively, mix your own hues:

1 On the slab, place about a teaspoonful of the palest colour in your mix.

2 Add tiny amounts of other hues. For example, to create lilac, begin with a base of white and add minute amounts of red (to achieve pink) and then even smaller quantities of blue to modify pink to lilac. N.B. Do not mix oil- and water-based inks together.

3 Do not add light colours to darker ones as you will waste vast amounts of the lighter shades to modify dark ones.

4 Mix ink by folding it over and over on the slab with a palette knife.

5 When you think you have the desired colour, dab a tiny blob onto white paper and spread thinly with a fingertip.

6 Continue to dab out samples between mixings until you are happy with the colour.

7 If the end hue is not critical and speed is essential (especially in class), simply roller out the dollops of colour on the slab quickly, changing rolling direction frequently, so each ink blob becomes fully mixed with the others.

Cardboard collage block showing a London bus, inked and ready for printing

Extending ink

To get translucent effects, the opacity of printing inks must be reduced with a medium or extender, which comes in tubes like the inks. Buy a variety consistent with your ink – oil-based, water-based, or oil-based water-washable. Reducing medium increases an ink's transparency without changing its consistency. Where layers of reduced colours overlap, new hues are created. So, for an image involving three partially overlapping colours, you could end up with a seven-colour print. Mix extended colour as described above – treating the extender as the lightest 'colour' and adding small amounts of opaque hues to it.

Rolling ink on the slab

1 The ink should be about as thick as toothpaste; usually, printing ink squeezed straight from the tube is the ideal consistency.

2 If there is an initial dribble of oil or water (depending on the ink used), wipe this away with kitchen towel and ink the slab as usual.

3 Ink that is too thick will not roll easily. To thin it, on the slab, add a drop of copperplate oil to oil-based ink or a drop of washing-up liquid to water-based ink.

4 Smear a small dollop of ink across the slab with the knife. To start, you need only the equivalent of one brush-worth of toothpaste but add more, at regular intervals, as needed.

5 When the ink is evenly rolled (which takes seconds) it looks like matt satin and the roller, moving across it, should make a gentle hiss rather than a squelching sound. There should be no lumps or areas of thicker ink – the surface should be completely smooth.

6 Don't ink the entire slab – a rolled square with sides roughly equal to the roller's width is ample. Rolling a wider area gives you more to clean later and wastes ink.

Inking a printing block

Some softer printers such as sponges, corks, broccoli florets and Plasticine blocks can be pressed by hand onto the slab to pick up ink. Other harder blocks, such as wood or card, need to be inked by roller or dabber.

Red London Bus by Year 2 child. Two-plate cereal box card print on white Somerset Satin paper. The background plate was inked in a green/blue blend; the 'bus' plate was inked in red

1 If the block is small, hold it in your hand to ink it.

2 If it is bigger and will lie flat, lay it on an ink-free surface and roll ink onto it.

3 Don't press hard; it is better to roll lightly so as not to distort a fragile block or squeeze ink into its delicate indentations.

4 Roll ink onto it from several directions to ensure it is evenly inked.

5 Now hold it to the light – it should glisten evenly all over. If you see any dull, matt areas, either apply more ink or roll out what is already there more evenly on the block. Practice will show you how much or how little to apply.

Making a colour blend

One way to create a multi-coloured print from one block is by colour blending in which two (or more) colours are blended on the slab, then rolled onto the block. Colour blending can be used to print blocks such as wood, lino, polystyrene, card and collage blocks; it can also be used when printing through stencils or for monotypes. Follow these steps to make a two-colour blend:

1 Take a clean roller a bit wider than your printing block.

2 Place two blobs of ink, each of a different hue (adding extender, if desired, for translucent effects) on a clean slab, one at each end of the roller's width.

3 With two palette knives, gently smear a line of ink inwards from each blob until the colours meet.

4 Roll back and forth with the roller across the smeared line until the ink is evenly rolled. The two colours will blend in the middle.

5 Unlike single-colour inking, do not change the rolling direction or the blend will be destroyed!

6 When inking a block with a blend, be sure to roll the block too in only one direction.

PRINTING THE INKED BLOCK

Hand-pressure

If the printer is small and not too hard – for instance cork, potato, sponge, broccoli floret, Plasticine or eraser – it can be printed simply by pressing by hand, inked-side-down, onto paper.

Spoon-burnishing

If the printer is more rigid (for instance, a coin, polystyrene, card or lino block), lay it inked-side-up on a clean surface, lay the printing paper down on top, then carefully burnish, through the back of the paper, with a teaspoon, as if making a brass rubbing (while holding the paper down with your other hand to prevent it from shifting and blurring the image). Carefully peel up a corner of the paper to check how the block is printing. If the impression is faint, lower the paper back in place and carry on rubbing. This process is known as spoon- or hand-burnishing. It is very effective but can be time-consuming. For most of the projects described, printing was carried out quite speedily by hand or roller pressure.

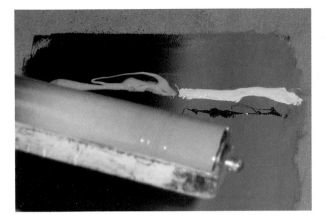

ABOVE LEFT Topping up a colour blend with fresh ink on the slab. The original blend was made with deep blue ink on the left and smears of red and white (to create pink) on the right. The blue side was too dark so no more blue ink is used to top it up. Instead, while a generous amount of white and a tiny smear of red ink are used to top up the right side of the blend, on the left a generous squeeze of compatible extender is used to

render the original blue less dense and more translucent. The roller is used to roll the blend (in one direction only) until the fresh ink is fully integrated into the existing blend

ABOVE RIGHT Rolling a cereal box card block with a colour blend, taking care to roll in only one direction so as not to muddy the blend

Year 2 child holding up her freshly-printed cereal box card print, printed with a purple/lilac ink blend. She and her class went on to create and print a second block over the first printing to create another layer of image and colour in their finished prints. Behind her can be seen classmates' cereal box card prints, in a blue/yellow blend, pegged on a line to dry

27

Roller printing

Lino, polystyrene and cardboard blocks can easily be printed by roller. Make sure the table on which you place the inked block is absolutely clean, prior to laying the paper on top, otherwise dirt or ink may be transferred, via roller printing, from table-top to paper. Now take a clean, hard roller and simply roll it firmly, half a dozen times, over the back of the paper. Hold the paper in place while you roll or it may slip. Ensure the roller makes contact with every part of the block, through the paper, as anything you miss will not print.

Troubleshooting

If the printed impression looks faint or if the paper is not sticking well to the inked block, either the block is too lightly inked or the ink is drying and you should roll out fresh ink onto both slab and block and reprint. If you over-ink the block and find that fine details are filling in, print two or three more impressions, without re-inking, onto scrap paper and/or press a clean pounce or a ball of Blu-Tack® over the block to lift out the excess ink; then re-ink the block for printing as usual.

ABOVE LEFT A red/yellow colour blend of Caligo™ water-washable oil-based ink was used to ink Year 3's polystyrene block prints. Here, a pale green sheet of Canford paper has been laid on the freshly-inked block and the back of the printing paper is rolled, with a clean rubber roller, to print it

ABOVE RIGHT Peeling off the finished print from the polystyrene block. The final picture is a mirror image of the drawing on the block

Inking and printing checklist

1 Place small dollop of ink on slab using colour from tube; or mix your own colour, add extender or prepare colour blend.

2 Roll out ink to a smooth even consistency.

3 Apply ink to printing block by roller, dabber or by pressing block straight into it.

4 Press inked mini-block directly on paper for printing or lay paper face down onto inked block and print by burnishing with roller, spoon or hand.

Kite flying on Parliament Hill by Year 3 child. Polystyrene block print in a red/yellow ink blend on purple Canford paper

3 Classroom management and cleaning up

CLASSROOM MANAGEMENT

With the exception of linocutting, which I would avoid at ages younger than Year 6, every other technique described could be carried out effectively by children from Nursery Class upwards. I would, however, advise against undertaking any of the whole-class projects described without having at least three adults in the classroom. As an artist, whilst I can impart enthusiasm and printing skills to children, I would rather leave the classroom management to their teachers who work with them every day!

My project involved 20 printing sessions – two or three per class, each being either a morning (9.30am to midday) or an afternoon (about 1.30 to 3pm), plus two evening inset sessions to introduce school staff to a variety of printing skills. The age range of each class was as follows: Nursery Class (age 3-4); Reception (age 4-5); Year 1 (age 5-6); Year 2 (age 6-7); Year 3 (age 7-8); Year 4 (age 8-9); Year 5 (age 9-10); Year 6 (age 10-11). With the exception of the Nursery Class (in which it proved most effective to work with three or four children at a time, in 15-minute sessions, in their classroom) all other classes were taught to groups of 30 in the artroom. Although that worked well, it required a high level of concentration to keep every child focused and everyone working at the same speed to get one or sometimes two projects completed per session. With only a few exceptions I aimed to start and finish a project within each two and a half or one and a half hour session (leaving at least half an hour for cleaning up). If my project hadn't had the goals of: a) teaching each class as many techniques as possible and b) making two substantial books of children's prints, all in a relatively short time, I might have approached each session differently. Perhaps I would have chosen to work with just 15 children per class over the first half of a session and the rest in the second half, aiming to complete one project with each smaller group in that time, rather than two projects with a larger group over the same hours. There is no right or wrong approach. Much depends on how many staff and assistants you have, how big a workspace and how much you wish to accomplish in a given time. I learned some useful classroom basics:

Group of Reception Class children experimenting with assorted printers including broccoli florets, the textured tyres of toy digger trucks and DIY blocks comprising variously textured materials stuck onto toy bricks. This was an unstructured printmaking activity running concurrently with a more complex task to keep everyone fully occupied throughout the lesson

BELOW Pencil study of Canary Wharf Tower, by Year 1 child, in preparation for a polystyrene block print of the same subject. If classes are able to go on sketching outings in advance of printing sessions, results are richer because the children have stronger and more personal visual imagery with which to work

1 The more adult assistance the better. Whilst I worked largely unaided in the Nursery (with small groups of children), managing other classes of 30 in complex, step-by-step, creative activities, involves much more strategic planning. For each whole-class session, you need at least three adults: a class teacher and two assistants (who could be school staff and/or parents).

2 Morning sessions are more productive than afternoons. The afternoon session is shorter, plus children seem less able to concentrate. With staff agreement, I quickly switched to mornings only. As a teacher you may not have that option but, as an artist coming to a school with a particular brief, it may make a big difference!

3 Discuss every project in advance with the class teacher in case (s)he may foresee snags or suggest improvements.

4 Plan each lesson carefully; the stages in making a print are a lot to take in for those new to it. I started every class by showing one or more examples, that I (or my own children) prepared in advance, of the type of print we were to make that day, then demonstrated, step by step, each stage of making it.

5 Have a theme. It focuses minds and can be linked with topics in the curriculum – e.g., healthy eating, road safety or local history.

6 Before embarking on a printmaking session, especially if it has a theme – be it buildings, landscapes, plant life, animals, shape and colour, figures etc. – each class should go sketching or take photos or look for magazine or internet images to build up a stock of ideas.

7 Bring books of artists' prints or actual examples (photocopies are fine) to inspire the class. When you've done some whole-class printing, you can use examples of prints from one class to inspire children in another. (If you don't want these to get spoiled, use photocopies or tidy them away before you uncap any ink tubes.)

8 Break down each technique into stages. This helps children to focus and maintains structure and momentum in the lesson. Stop the class as each step is completed and explain and/or demonstrate what to do next.

9 Prepare a demonstration print in advance (if you have children at home, enlist their help). This will help you work through any snags and give a good idea of how long each stage might take. In class, keep these timings in mind so you can be sure to finish on time.

10 At the start of each session, have everything you need to hand (make a list in advance). I prepared a table on which rollers, inks, papers, pencils, blocks, sponges, etc., were laid out (in separate plastic tubs) and on which I demonstrated techniques. It is easy to find what you want if everything is in one place and this will also help you keep control of your tools and materials.

11 Have a bowl or sink of warm soapy water ready from the outset; it's surprising how quickly you need it! Also make sure you have old newspapers handy, as well as everything else you will need for the clean up.

Classroom assistant pegging Year 2 cereal box card prints to dry, straight away after printing, so that they are not damaged by being left on inky tables. Each child wrote their name in pencil on the back of the printing paper, prior to printing, for ease of identification and distribution later

12 Before any ink is rolled, ensure every child rolls up their sleeves to the elbow or higher and puts on an apron or adult-size old T-shirt to protect their clothes.

13 Before you start printing, string up a washing line to peg up wet prints straight away and ensure that everyone pegging the prints has clean hands. Prints left lying around are at risk of being dropped on the floor or getting inky fingermarks on them.

14 Make sure you have plenty of printing paper ready at the start of each lesson; once classes start to print they get through it exceedingly fast.

15 Ensure that an adult or responsible child controls paper distribution. It is all too easy, especially if the stack of printing paper is multi-coloured, for chilren with inky fingers to rifle through it for a favourite colour and inadvertently spoil the whole lot. For the same reason, keep the stack well away from wet ink and rollers.

16 Plan ahead. Generally speaking, the younger children worked much faster than I had initially anticipated. A polystyrene-block printing session that I had envisaged would take Year 1 a whole morning, for instance, only saw them through to morning break. So, have more activities up your sleeve to fill time.

17 Consider class size. With enough time and assistants, it might be more efficient to work with half rather than a whole class and, while one half embarks on a printing activity, the other, in another room, continues with regular lessons; then groups could swap over halfway through.

18 For younger children, try to have at least two activities (one more complex and one simple) running concurrently so that if any finish a stage of the complex project faster than others, they can move to another table for a simple hand-printing task that will keep them busy whilst classmates catch up. Also, if adult helpers are few, those available can concentrate on supervising the complex task while the simpler activity (printing 'trees' from cut halves of broccoli florets for instance) can almost look after itself.

19 Teach helping adults some specific techniques so that they can take control of some of the children's printmaking and thus feel confident enough to pursue printmaking in class without you.

20 Keep inking slabs and rollers under adult control. Children love squeezing ink out of tubes, rolling it onto any surface in sight and sticking fingers or clothes into it! They will enjoy this but, if you are trying to get any result other than a phenomenal waste of ink that will take hours to clean, I advise against allowing a class

Year 6 cutting small lino blocks. On the tables, they have the same preparatory drawings and photographs to work from that they had used for an earlier monotype printing session. The same visual reference material can be used many times to make different prints

Year 5 children inking lino blocks for printing. The children learned a great deal by inking their own blocks, greatly enjoyed the experience and produced many prints, but the prints' quality was poorer than when working with one child at a time

to do the ink-rolling – unless you can supervise each child. It may be more practical for adults to do roller-inking but let children, with supervision, do the printing. It is especially important to keep control of the roller if you have prepared a colour blend; rolling in the wrong direction will instantly spoil it.

21 Enlist adults to keep slabs topped up with ink and to ink blocks that need roller- or dabber-inking. When a class is doing its own printing, especially using sponges, the ink is used up at an astonishing rate and needs constant replenishment. If embarking on a print in stages, get the children to wash their hands before each new colour is commenced; the final results will be much cleaner and, if you have limited numbers of slabs and rollers, this will give you vital minutes to clean those up before re-inking in a fresh colour. It also keeps the speedier children occupied whilst classmates catch up.

22 Ensure each child writes his/her name on each print before it is hung up to dry as, being reversals of images on their blocks, children sometimes find it hard to identify their own work a few days later.

23 Sometimes, especially when working with a textured printer (e.g., a child's toy brick with bubble-wrap stuck to it), children get over-enthusiastic in their printing so that an image that commences with clearly visible printed textures quickly deteriorates into a muddy mess. While not wanting to be too prescriptive, be watchful and intervene to stop a child adding to an image if you think more printing will spoil it. Give the child fresh paper to work on to keep up his/her enthusiasm while rescuing their interesting print from being tested to destruction!

24 Allow at least half an hour at the end of a session for cleaning up and, if possible, get the children to help. Some can start cleaning up while others are finishing their work.

25 Be flexible and don't panic! If your project isn't going as planned, remember that half the fun of printmaking is the surprise of its results. Be prepared to change and adapt in response to the work the children produce or how much time you have available. Flexibility often makes for a better print than you could have anticipated.

26 Printmaking produces surprising, often unexpected, results that adults and children find exciting. In the midst of the sheer logistics of getting everyone's print printed and trying not to wreak inky havoc in the classroom, remember to enjoy it!

The author demonstrating to a class how *not* to cut lino; she is cutting with her right hand while her left hand rests on the block, directly in the blade's path

End of a Year 5 linocutting and printing session. The wet prints have been pegged on a line to dry (and some are also spread on a clean table as the line was not long enough for them all). The class is helping to tidy the workroom. One boy is sweeping the floor clean of lino shavings

CLEANING UP

1 Have bin bags taped to worktables throughout each lesson for the ongoing disposal of recyclable waste (inky paper or newspapers etc.) and another refuse sack for any non-recyclable waste. The printing inks recommended are all non-toxic so inky papers can safely be recycled.

2 Rub barrier cream onto your hands before printing; ink (whether oil or water-based) will then easily wash off your skin with water. Alternatively, wear rubber or latex gloves.

3 After printing, use a palette knife to scrape excess ink from the slab. Wipe it onto newspaper and dispose of it in the binbag taped to your worktable. Wipe the knife clean on newspaper, rags or kitchen roll.

4 If you use water-based or water-washable inks, ink slabs, rollers and hands can all be cleaned effectively with undiluted liquid soap, washing-up liquid or warm soapy water. If you use oil-based ink, this can be shifted with a generous dollop of vegetable oil rubbed into the ink with rag or paper towel, followed by cleaning with washing-up liquid and warm water.

5 Don't use knives to scrape ink off rollers as they may scratch a roller's smooth surface; wipe off ink splashes from rollers' sides and frames. Relatively cheap rollers, especially those with plastic handles, can be left to soak for an hour or two in hot soapy water if water-based/water-washable ink proves hard to shift.

6 Perishable blocks such as fruit or vegetable printers should be thrown away after printing (ideally in a compost bin). Fragile blocks such as Plasticine can be left to dry; attempts at cleaning are likely to distort their surfaces. Cardboard and collage blocks too, if not sealed with PVA, should be left to dry naturally as cleaning will cause them to disintegrate. Lino blocks can be left to dry naturally or washed in soapy water (provided inking was done with water-based/water-washable ink). The surface of polystyrene blocks, however, sometimes perishes with cleaning so is best avoided. DIY printing blocks – such as children's building bricks with a printing surface made with bubble wrap or corrugated card stuck to one side – can be left to dry naturally or washed clean, with care, but the printing surface may well perish and need replacing, whether cleaned or not; these blocks are quick and easy to make and repair so don't worry about them. Blocks that have been left uncleaned, to dry naturally, will print perfectly well another time, but be careful to reprint using the same or a darker colour, as the older ink residue may be re-activated by the fresh ink and affect the colour of the next printing.

View from Victoria Park by Year 5 child. Linocut printed in white ink on black Canford paper

4 *Monotypes with pencils and cotton buds*

A monotype is a one-off print: a unique impression printed from glass, Perspex® (Plexiglas), metal, card or any other smooth surface. The freshly-inked slab with an image drawn or rubbed into it serves as the printing block but the resulting print cannot be repeated exactly as it is not made from a block (or any other semi-permanent printing matrix). For this reason, monotype is perhaps less versatile than other print processes, since the image cannot be repeated (except to take increasingly pale impressions from the ink residue left after the initial printing). One-off prints do, however, have particular, sometimes painterly, qualities and are quick, easy and satisfying to make. For all monotype methods, you must work fairly quickly so the ink does not dry before you have finished – but this is not a problem with primary-school-age children who take between one and 15 minutes maximum (a sliding scale dependent on age – youngest working fastest) to create monotype images.

Reception Class children drawing designs, using cotton buds, into wet ink rolled on wipe-clean white boards that served as individual ink slabs for every child. When the drawings were complete, a piece of lightweight Japanese printing paper was laid in place on each wet ink drawing and carefully rubbed by hand to transfer ink to paper and create a (wiping method) monotype print

My house by Reception Class child. Monotype (wiping method) drawn with cotton bud in a blend of green/blue ink, printed on Japanese paper

In the classroom I used Caligo™ oil-based water-washable inks for all monotype techniques described and they performed wonderfully well. In my own studio I use regular oil-based inks, which work equally well. Water-based inks seem to work less well for this process because they dry too quickly and can cause paper to cockle.

WIPING METHOD

This is a quick and easy technique and produces vividly coloured, lively, painterly images. I taught it to Reception Class and Year 1 but it is suitable for all ages.

1 Each child needs their own individually inked slab. You could roll each slab with a single colour or a two-colour blend.

2 To prepare slabs fast, roll out the blend first on one slab, then use that slab to charge the roller with ink for all subsequent slabs. The first slab will probably need replenishing after each six or seven

slabs have been prepared from it but this is still quicker than creating a fresh slab, with ink direct from the tubes, for each child.

3   Each slab should be inked as if you were going to use it for inking and printing a block but, in this instance, the slab itself becomes the printing block, so, keep its inking to a neat rectangle.

4   If the inked shape looks untidy, edge it with a border of masking tape to 'frame' it cleanly.

5   To make the image, draw directly into the wet ink. Marks can be made with assorted implements: from a fine pencil-line, to a scratchy old paintbrush, to (most dramatically) the broad, sweeping lines made by rubbing or wiping with a cotton bud, finger or rag. Try dragging a comb or fork prongs through the ink or running a toy car's tyres across it.

6   If printing on white paper, remember that the marks you make will be the white areas of the print, which will be a mirror-image of the drawing on the slab – so numbers or letters should be drawn in reverse.

7   If small children want to include numbers or letters, it helps to draw these out on tracing paper, then turn the tracing over and use the reversed image as a guide to copy on to the monotype slab.

8   If you want the marks you draw or wipe to comprise the dark parts of the print, then ink the slab in a pale, opaque (i.e., not extended) colour, draw the image and print it on dark-hued paper.

Tower and boat by Year 1 child. Monotype (wiping method) drawn with cotton bud in a blend of blue/yellow ink, printed on yellow Nepalese Lhokta paper

9 When the image is complete and before the ink starts to dry, lay a clean sheet of smooth paper onto it. Press it in place with your hand; if it is fairly thin and the ink reasonably tacky, it will stick in place. If the paper is thicker and the ink beginning to dry, it helps to tape the paper lightly with masking tape, along two sides, so it doesn't slip during printing.

10 Print by rubbing the back of the paper with the palm or side of your hand or else roll it with a clean roller or rub with a spoon. From time to time, lift a corner to check whether the image has transferred. If the paper is semi-transparent, the image will show clearly through the back, as you rub.

11 When it has printed to your satisfaction, carefully peel off any tape, lift off the finished print and hang it up to dry. This whole printing process takes barely a minute.

Monotypes with 4-6-year-olds

When making wiped monotypes with Reception Class and Year 1 children, we printed on semi-transparent, Japanese papers because these stuck firmly to the ink and made using tape unnecessary, were strong enough to withstand printing without tearing and the children found it exciting seeing their images appear through the back of the paper as they rubbed. Also, as the paper was so thin, it didn't absorb all the ink off the slabs, so it was possible, after the first printing, to lay a second sheet in place on each slab and rub it to gain a paler, but still effective, 'ghost print' (see p.46) of the same image.

Chinese Dragon by Year 2 child. Monotype (drawing method) on pale blue Thai handmade paper

In these examples, children had been asked to draw monotype images of their house, flat or any London landmark. Year 1 made drawings in advance, which proved immensely useful. All the children greatly enjoyed using cotton buds: they found it hilarious yet intriguing that a cotton bud could be used for drawing; it fits comfortably in small hands so they were all immediately very confident drawing with it; and a cotton bud makes a fairly broad, sweeping line in the ink, which encourages children not to work at too tiny a scale but to fill the whole slab with their drawing.

The total time for 30 children to produce one monotype was about an hour per class. Most of that time was spent preparing and distributing slabs rolled with a two-colour blend and cleaning hands and slabs afterwards. Whilst waiting for their inked slabs, the children made sketches on scrap paper of ideas for their prints. The actual time making and printing monotypes was barely ten minutes but the activity was immensely rewarding.

DRAWING METHOD

This is a quick, effective way of creating fine-lined drawings with attractive random tone. It is a technique used by well-known artists including Paul Klee (1879-1940). Monotype drawings can look similar to etchings with attractive qualities of line and tone.

1 Using a minute quantity of ink (about half of what you would use to prepare a slab for inking a block), roll out a really thin ink layer into a neat shape on the slab. The ink should have a smooth, satiny look with no dust or fluff in it. (Oil-based water-washable ink is ideal for this as it stays wet longer than water-based.)

2 Mask off irregular inky edges with a frame of masking tape.

3 Select a sheet of paper a bit larger than the inked rectangle and place it so it completely covers the inked surface. (Both cheap and expensive papers take excellent monotype drawings.)

Chinese dragon by Year 2 child. Monotype (drawing method) on yellow Thai handmade paper

4 Tape the paper down lightly on at least two sides, so it won't shift while you're drawing.

5 Cut a sheet of tracing paper to roughly the same size as the printing paper and lay it on top to cover (and protect) it. Tape this down along the same two edges.

6 Draw an image onto the back of the tracing paper with medium-hard pencil. The pencil's pressure will transfer the wet ink from slab to printing paper.

7 Alternatively, prepare the image in advance on tracing paper, then lay the tracing over the back of the printing paper and, with a pencil, carefully go over the lines of your drawing to transfer it via the wet ink on the slab onto the printing paper.

8 When the drawing is complete, carefully peel off all tape and peel the print off the slab. The printed drawing will have an attractive furry-line quality and there will be soft tonal areas where ink has transferred to the paper, relating to where your hand rested on the back of it when you were drawing.

9 If the ink on the slab is too thick, the drawing may come out darker than you'd expected. If this happens, you may still get a satisfactory result by laying fresh paper on the slab and pulling a 'ghost' print (see p.46) from it before you clean up; alternatively (or subsequently) roll out the ink again (without adding more from the tube) to create a fresh, slightly less inky surface on which to make a new monotype.

Monotypes of China Town

I introduced Year 2 and Year 6 children to the 'drawing method' of monotype, which they all enjoyed – but it is a technique that can be accomplished by anyone from about age 4 upwards. Year 2's subject was London's China Town to which, in advance, they made a trip to make sketches and take photos. As with the wiping method described, the most time was spent preparing and distributing ink slabs (here inked with black ink), leaving only 15 or 20 minutes for drawing and printing to take place – so it was helpful that each child had a drawing or photo to work from, so that they could all start to draw straightaway without wasting valuable time deciding what to draw.

Toner cartridge monotypes

If you haven't time to ink up and clean so many slabs, excellent and very speedy drawing monotypes can be made by recycling the used toner paper (A4 sheets) from Riso, multi-copier, duplicator machines or also by using sheets of carbon copy paper. You simply:

RIGHT *Lines of frying ducks in Chinese restaurant* by Year 2 child. Monotype (drawing method) on red Nepalese Lhokta paper. Photo © Madeleine Waller 2008

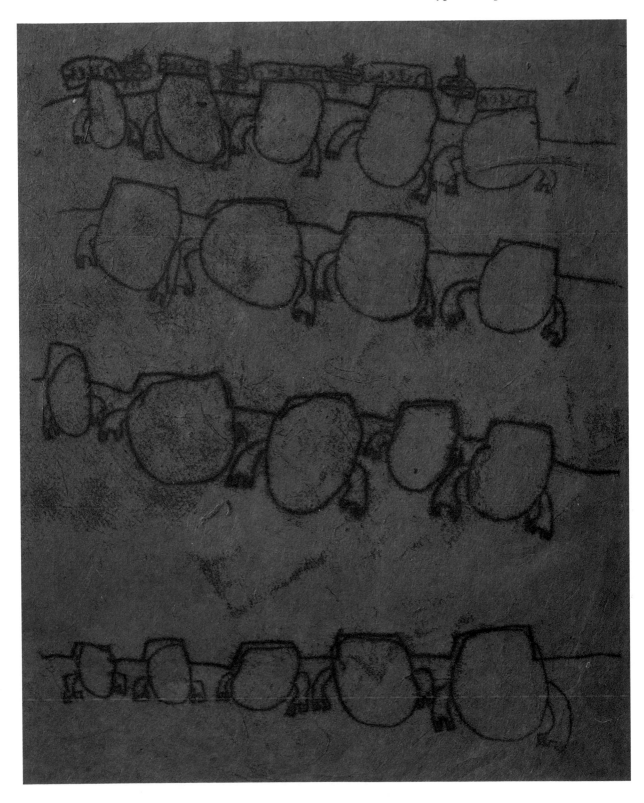

1 Lay a sheet of clean printing paper on the worktop.
2 Place the toner paper, toner-side-down on top.
3 Lay tracing (or any other scrap paper) on top.
4 Draw on the tracing or scrap paper with hard pencil.
5 Peel away tracing and toner paper to reveal finished print.

Monotypes of London landmarks

Year 6's subject was London landmarks; they had prepared by taking photos of the neighbourhood. I supplemented these with some of my own, as well as some of my wood engraved prints of architectural subjects – all of which gave them a range of ideas for their own prints. Year 6 had a morning session of monotypes (about two and a half hours). In that time, they made some preparatory sketches on rough paper before trying out drawing, wiping and ghost monotype printing to good effect.

The British Museum by Year 6 child. Monotype (drawing method) in black and yellow blended ink on white, semi-transparent, Japanese paper. This monotype came out so black that the image was obscured. However, through the back of the printing paper, the image showed through clearly while the strong black tone was muted to subtle grey. So, in this instance, the back of the print became the front

ABOVE *British Museum series: No 1* by Anne Desmet. Wood engraving printed in black ink on Japanese Gampi Vellum paper. Image size: 17.4x24.8cm. Several Year 6 monotypes and linocuts were directly inspired by this image

LEFT *The British Museum, Great Court library and glass roof* by Year 6 child. Monotype (drawing method) in black and yellow blended ink on white, semi-transparent, Japanese paper

GHOST PRINTING

A 'ghost print' is a term used to describe any subsequent prints pulled from an already printed ink slab, before the residue of the drawing in the wet ink has been cleaned up or before the slab has been rolled with a fresh ink layer. These prints, having less ink on them than the first printing, will be paler, more ghostly versions than the first. Ghost prints can be particularly striking when pulled from the ink residue of a 'drawing method' monotype. With the drawing method, the drawing comes out in the darkest tones (assuming you used a dark-coloured ink) that stands out against a pale paper background. But if you make a ghost print of this type of monotype the effect is like a ghostly photo negative; all the detail prints crisply, but what were formerly dark lines in the initial print become paper white, whilst the previously pale background tones become the darkest areas of the new print. Ghost prints pulled from the ink residue of a 'wiping method' monotype simply appear as paler variants of the first print pulled. To print a 'ghost' impression: as soon as a first monotype has been pulled, tape a fresh sheet of printing paper on the wet slab and rub with your hand, or roll firmly with a clean roller, across the back of the paper, to transfer the slab's ink residue to the paper.

ABOVE LEFT *The British Museum, Great Court* by Year 6 child. Monotype (drawing method) in red-brown and blue blended ink on Japanese Kozu-shi paper

ABOVE RIGHT *The British Museum, Great Court* by the same Year 6 child. Monotype ghost print created from the wet ink residue of the first monotype drawing. Between the pulling of the first monotype and this ghost print, a few drops of yellow ink were accidentally splashed onto the slab. These can be seen in this ghost print but don't detract from its impact

5 *Polystyrene blocks from pizza trays*

Flat pieces of polystyrene (styro foam) of the type used for take-away burger boxes make great printing blocks. Wipe the box clean, then cut out the flat, rectangular top and bottom pieces; these will be your blocks. Much bigger, circular pieces are also found in pizza packaging. You can also buy 'Poly board' sheets, specially for printing, from art materials shops. Personally, I prefer to recycle polystyrene pizza trays for printing. When cut up, you get three or four printing blocks from just one tray. I collected pizza packaging for several months before I taught this technique to Reception, Year 1, Year 2 and Year 3. At 30 polystyrene prints per class (or 120 different prints), each printed twice, we had 240 polystyrene block prints in all, made in sessions lasting no more than an hour and a half per class – and all made from recycled pizza trays! Polystyrene block printmaking is quick, easy and satisfying for children (and anyone else without the hand-strength for the cutting involved in relief print processes such as linocutting) and the prints retain the individuality and character of a lively drawing.

1 Draw firmly into the polystyrene using biro or hard (but not too sharp) pencil. It doesn't matter whether the biro leaves a mark, but it must leave an indentation. The dented marks should be deep enough to feel with a fingertip but you don't need to dig right through the board.

2 Customise the block's shape (if desired) by cutting off pieces with scissors.

3 Roll the block with ink. For printing polystyrene, water-washable oil-based ink works best. Water-based ink is repelled by the block's greasy surface and doesn't print well. Also, the block's surface begins to decay, quite quickly, when printed with water-based inks, but withstands more impressions – at least ten – when printed with oil-based.

4 During inking, thin or small blocks may lift off the worktop and wrap themselves around the roller. If this happens, drip a couple of drops of water onto a clean inking slab and press the block onto the surface, ready for re-inking. Ink up as normal. The water seals the block to the slab's surface, making rolling much easier.

5 To break the seal, slide a clean knife blade beneath the block.

6 Print by laying a smooth paper on top of the inked block (if there is stray ink on the slab near the inked block, you should move it to a clean surface for printing).

7 Pat the paper down so it adheres to the ink.

8 Burnish by rolling the back of the paper firmly with a clean roller before peeling print from block.

Younger children tend to produce tiny drawings that don't remotely fill the block. So, I gave each one a piece of scrap paper along with their block (the blocks, cut from pizza trays, came in assorted shapes and sizes). I asked each child to draw carefully around the edge of their polystyrene onto the scrap paper, then, lifting the polystyrene block away, they had a template of their block's shape on which to make a preliminary design, prior to indenting it on the block, and on which they could practise making their drawing fill the block. This sketch also allowed them to make a positive feature of each block's unusual shape.

Houses on a map

Each Reception Class child was asked to draw a picture of his/her home on the block. When finished, the adults assisted them to cut their blocks into house- or flat-like shapes. We inked the blocks and printed them onto pages from an out-of-date London A-Z map book.

LEFT Inking a polystyrene block

ABOVE The inked block ready for printing

RIGHT *My house* by Reception Class child. Polystyrene block printed in black ink on London A-Z map page

ABOVE LEFT Image indented on a polystyrene (pizza tray) block. This polystyrene's original colour was black; the block has not yet been inked

ABOVE CENTRE The freshly inked block is laid, inked side down, on the printing paper. (We found this the easiest way of aligning the block in a precise position on the paper; alternatively, you can lay the paper directly down on the inked block)

ABOVE RIGHT The block, ink and paper 'sandwich' is turned over so the paper is on top. Now the child rolls the back of the printing paper, with a clean roller, to print the block

LEFT The finished print: *My house* by Reception Class child. Polystyrene block printed in black ink on London A-Z map page

The map pages provided an apt context for these prints of the children's homes while adding a richly coloured, patterned contrast to our black printing ink. This also usefully recycled a redundant book!

From China Town to Parliament Hill

Year 1 children drew pictures of their homes or other East London buildings onto polystyrene blocks. Those in Year 2 drew London's China Town. Year 3 children created images of a day they spent kite-flying and sketching on London's Parliament Hill; these last were particularly successful when drawn on semi-circular sections of pizza tray as that shape suggested a panoramic horizon. All these classes had made plenty of preparatory drawings and taken photos, in advance of these sessions, that were invaluable source material for prints. I inked all these blocks with colour blends and printed them on coloured Canford paper. A few were printed on Nepalese Lhokta. The children really enjoyed the combination of bright, blended ink colours on vivid paper. Each polystyrene printing session, from drawing the image to printing it, took about an hour and a half per class.

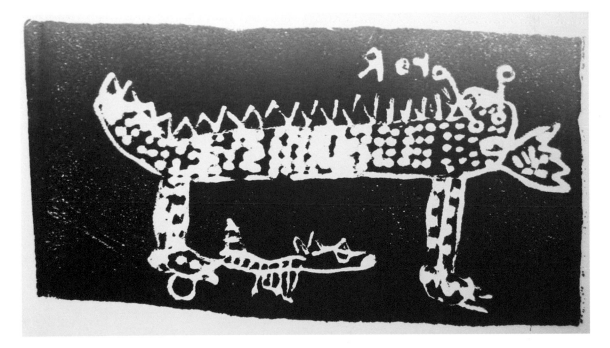

Chinese dragon by Year 2 child. Polystyrene block printed in a red/orange ink blend on pale blue Canford paper

51

Pencil drawing on white cartridge paper by Year 1 child. Preparatory study for polystyrene block print

Year 1 child holding polystyrene block indented with his drawing, ready for printing

BELOW The finished polystyrene block print in a green/yellow ink blend on red Canford paper

RIGHT Photograph of the Chinese Gate, China Town, London, with the Post Office Tower visible in the distance. This was taken by the class teacher as reference material on a Year 2 sketching trip where the class made drawings in preparation for printmaking

BELOW LEFT *Chinese Gate* by Year 2 child. Polystyrene block print in a red/orange ink blend on turquoise blue Canford paper

BELOW RIGHT *Chinese Gate and Post Office Tower* by Year 2 child. Polystyrene block print in a red/orange ink blend on turquoise blue Canford paper. Photo © Madeleine Waller 2008

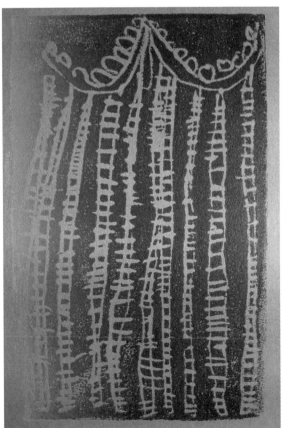

Chinese Gate by the author's daughter, Marion in Year 2. Polystyrene block print in a blue/green ink blend on orange Canford paper

ABOVE Polystyrene block (section of round, black pizza tray) indented with a design and inked for printing

RIGHT Year 3 artist examining a print (on white cartridge paper) pulled from this same polystyrene block

BELOW *View from Parliament Hill* by Year 3 child. Polystyrene block print in a red/yellow blend on blue Canford paper

6 DIY printing blocks for texture and pattern

More or less anything with at least one flattish surface can be used as a printer: eggboxes, the round ends of cardboard tubes, wine-bottle corks, keys, ice-lolly sticks, dried pasta, Plasticine, bottle lids, old toothbrushes, plastic fridge-magnet letters and numbers, dried leaves, textured wood or bark, stone or slate, shoe soles, sponges, seashells, toy cars (look for textured tyres), and wooden or plastic toy bricks.

Children's building bricks are especially useful as supports for making DIY, customised printing blocks. These blocks are quick and easy to make, and can be used again and again; they are easy to repair or replace, are easy to hold and print and can add fascinating textures and details to images of every kind.

Making a DIY block

1 Use double-sided sticky tape to cover one flat surface of the toy brick.

2 Stick something printable onto it. All these work well: bubble-wrap, mesh/netting, corrugated cardboard, shapes cut from smooth cardboard, foam rubber/card shapes (that you can buy for collage), textured polystyrene, smooth pieces of polystyrene (that you can cut to a shape and/or indent with a design), embossed wallpaper, paper doilies, crumpled paper or tinfoil, textured fabric (including woven or knitted pieces, crochet-work or lace).

3 Trim any overhang so that nothing sticks out beyond the edges of the brick.

4 Alternatively, try sticking flat buttons, paper-clips, coins or feathers onto its surface.

5 Wire, furry pipe-cleaners, string and elastic bands can be wrapped around a brick; they stick well to the double-sided tape on the printing face and survive several printing sessions if secured, in addition, with masking tape at the back and sides.

6 Make as many of these DIY blocks as you can using lots of different textures. Inevitably, some won't withstand the rough handling they get, so the more you prepare the better!

Lots of houses by Nursery Class child. Printed in green and black inks using the DIY toy brick printer with corrugated card house design – shown on extreme left of image on facing page

You can also make good printing blocks from vegetables and fruit such as cauliflower, broccoli, mushrooms, potatoes, swedes, carrots, turnips, apples or starfruit. These blocks don't store well. They grow mould or shrivel within a couple of days, so print the day after you make them, then compost them.

Most DIY printers, while reasonably resilient, need to be treated with care. Children love the spontaneity and speed of simply pressing the textured surface into ink, then pressing the printer, by hand, straight onto paper. They quickly realize it is not even strictly necessary to re-ink between printings as you can achieve successful, increasingly pale impressions from a block by continuing to print from it, straight away, without re-inking. The one drawback to these blocks is that, however much you tell children simply to 'dab, dab, dab' them in ink, in their enthusiasm, some DIY blocks get 'scrubbed' in it instead. That quickly causes the printable texture to

Collection of DIY toy brick (and wine-bottle cork) printers with textures including: bubble wrap; corrugated card; textured polystyrene; piece of crocheted doily; collage-foam cut into specific shapes; fabric mesh; string; and pipe cleaner

become detached. Children are much more likely to 'scrub' if the slab's ink is running low, so the problem is less likely to occur if you keep slabs well topped up with fresh ink.

DIY skylines and gift wrap

I initially created a biscuit-tin-full of about 40 such DIY blocks, with a range of textured surfaces, in preparation for printing with Nursery Class. In advance, I prepared a large tracing paper stencil showing an invented skyline but featuring, in outline, some recognisable London buildings. (But the technique, as with all others described, could be applied to any subject matter or age group.) The drawing on the tracing paper stretched from one side of the paper to the other so, when carefully cut along the drawn line, the tracing paper parted in two, each part being a separate stencil. The upper part was designed to cover the intended 'sky' area of a large piece of deep blue-green-coloured Lhokta paper to which I attached it with Blu-tack®. In class I prepared two slabs, one with red, one with yellow ink (chosen as they would show up

City skyline by Nursery Class. Large stencil print printed with sponges (in white ink) and DIY toy brick printers (in red and yellow inks) on blue-green Nepalese Lhokta paper, image size: 49x63cm

strongly against the dark paper) and laid these on opposite sides of the Lhokta paper. I put half a dozen DIY blocks out on each slab and positioned one or two children per slab. Working with just three or four children at a time, with 10 or 15 minutes per group, I asked them to print the DIY blocks all over the Lhokta paper – wherever they chose (the stencil protecting the top section of printing paper). They also enjoyed printing more DIY blocks in other colours on smaller, A4-sized sheets of white cartridge paper. After an hour, most of the class had printed some individual prints as well as adding layers of textural printing to the large sheet of paper.

I then laid the second stencil on the paper, matching it up exactly with the contour of the first and covering all printing the children had already done on this sheet. I stuck it down with Blu-tack® before peeling off the first stencil to reveal the unprinted 'sky'. I rolled out cream-coloured ink (white with a dash of yellow) onto a clean slab and gave the last child a sponge printer. She used this, with my help, to sponge-print the cream colour into the 'sky'. This provided a

River Thames at night by Year 2 child. Paper stencil print with sponge and various DIY printers printed in pink, cream, green and blue inks on white Somerset Satin paper (pre-rolled with purple ink)

59

Patterned paper (or gift wrap) by Lauriston School staff. Paper stencil print in pink, red, yellow and blue-black ink printed with sponges and DIY toy brick printers on a large sheet of white paper, 76x54cm

contrasting texture and colour and helped define clearly the stencilled outlines of buildings. Once the sky was printed – a few minutes work – several children helped peel off the stencil from the lower part of the print to reveal the finished work.

The act of peeling off a stencil to reveal a finished print is magical – it has a huge 'wow' factor. While the print was being printed it looked rather a mess but, when the second stencil was pulled away, suddenly there was a clearly defined image that tiny children had made; they found it amazing!

My DIY blocks proved incredibly versatile when working with many other age groups. Year 3 and the teaching staff, for instance, used them to create patterned papers that involved printing, with DIY blocks, through a stencil pattern of trees and simple buildings.

Patterned paper (or gift wrap) by Year 3. Paper stencil print (in red and blue ink) using DIY toy brick printers on a large sheet of white paper, 76x54cm, impregnated with blue flower petals

BELOW *House and tree* by Reception Class child. Using a similar stencil motif to the larger patterned papers illustrated, the area around the stencil has been printed in red with a sponge, then in black with a DIY textured polystyrene printer, on mustard-yellow Thai handmade paper

Night and day panoramas

Year 1 children used DIY printers to create two lengthy panoramic cityscapes depicting night and day. We divided the class into three groups. One group of seven or eight children each made a Plasticine printer in the form of a building, tree, animal or person, to be printed later. (For more on Plasticine printers, see Chapter 8.) The second group, also seven or eight children, simply experimented with printing assorted DIY and sponge printers on cartridge paper. As children in the first group finished their Plasticine models (which were moved to shelves and window ledges, out of the way), they swapped places with children in the second group until both groups had made their models and done some printing.

The third group of the rest of the class – 15 children – lined up along three trestle tables placed end-to-end in a continuous line. The tables were protected with brown paper and long, narrow strips of Somerset Satin 250gsm white printing paper were laid out on top.

(The strips were joined at the back with a self-adhesive paper tape, Filmoplast P90 – but an easier tactic would be to print on a roll of wallpaper lining paper, or an artists' paper that can be bought by the roll.) With the children's help, working directly with a roller charged with black ink, we rolled a black baseline along one edge of the paper. As we intentionally did not roll a straight line, the black roller mark on the paper tilted up and down, suggesting hills and valleys. I then removed the black ink slab and roller and replaced these with five new slabs, one rolled with red ink, a couple with yellow and a couple with extended blue. (The blue was extended to appear more translucent and paler on the paper than ink straight from the tube. This would make the 'buildings' print fainter, as if in the distance of our invented view.) On each slab I placed three DIY blocks (one per child, though they could swap blocks with one another as they pleased). The children were asked to treat the wavy black roller line as the 'ground' and print the DIY printers as if they were buildings growing up from it; broccoli was printed to look like trees between buildings. (Although I asked the children to imagine buildings 'growing' upwards out of the ground and print their blocks accordingly, some were printed horizontally across the paper or leaning in unsteady diagonals; the resulting scenes have a wild, dangerous look suggesting thunderstorms or fireworks!)

After about half an hour, when the first two groups had finished their Plasticine models and the third had filled the length of white printing paper with printed shapes and patterns that quickly developed the character of a cityscape, the groups were rotated so that group three now became groups one and two and vice versa – so

Year 1 beginning to print their 'Daytime' panorama on white Somerset Satin paper. The black 'baseline' created by rolling a wavy line with a freshly inked roller can clearly be seen. The children are just starting to print buildings and trees, in blue ink, using DIY toy brick printers and sliced broccoli florets respectively

every child took part in all three activities. As the 'daytime' print was now almost finished, it was pegged on the washing line while fresh strips of black paper, to make our 'night' panorama, were laid out. The former groups one and two (who had rotated to become the new group three) printed the 'ground' with an undulating rolled line of white ink – which looked like moonlit or snowy ground. I prepared fresh slabs with white, yellow and pink hues with a clean batch of 15 more DIY blocks, which the children used to print the nighttime buildings. (We could not re-use the first blocks as they had just been

BELOW Year 1 *Daytime panorama* (detail). Print created with variously textured DIY printing blocks (in paler colours) and Plasticine printers (in dark blue ink)

printed with darker inks that would have muddied these paler colours and there wasn't time to get the first batch washed and dried. Another time, I would start with the 'night' print, printing paler hues first, and print the 'day' second because you can print a dark colour using a block still wet with a paler hue and achieve a result within the darker tonal range you desire; but, if you try to print a light colour with a block still wet with a dark one, the result will be 'muddy'.

The final stage was to print the Plasticine printers onto the 'day' and 'night' prints. For this, the children of the current group three were given back their models (although we lost track of who had made what, so each child got a model to print but not necessarily their own!). Using dark blue ink, they printed them in the white 'ground' area of the 'night' print to suggest figures, animals, trees or buildings in the foreground, set against paler 'moonlit' structures behind. This group then went to wash their hands and remove protective overalls/T-shirts, while the remainder of the class printed their models in blue-black ink as a foreground to the 'day' print, before they too cleaned themselves up.

Many images in this book incorporate, amongst other methods, textures made by printing with these versatile sponge and DIY printers. I have since used them in my own prints and find them incredibly useful. Because I had only two or three printing sessions per class, I prepared all the DIY blocks myself. However, making their own blocks would be an interesting project for children and would extend their understanding of printmaking.

Year 1 printing their 'Nighttime' panorama on black paper. The white baseline created by rolling a wavy line with a freshly inked roller can clearly be seen. Children are printing buildings, in pink ink, using DIY toy brick printers

BELOW Year 1 *Nighttime panorama* (detail). Print created with variously textured DIY printing blocks (in pastel hues) and Plasticine printers (in dark blue ink)

7 Paper stencil prints and acetate 'stained glass'

Stencilling produces bold images with strongly defined outline shapes. You need: thin card, acetate or reasonably strong paper; pencil and scissors. Stencilling can be used to print on paper and other surfaces, flat or curved, such as acetate, glass, china, plastic, wood or textiles. A stencil simply masks out or protects one part of the print while you are printing another. I used stencils in many projects in school – sometimes as a stand-alone technique but more often mixing it with other processes such as linocut or Plasticine printing or DIY block-printing. As each stencil was only intended to withstand one printing session, we made them all on tracing or sugar paper and disposed of them afterwards. For greater durability, use thin card or acetate.

This chapter describes three projects for stencils printed with sponges or DIY blocks. Chapters 6, 8 and 11 include further projects involving stencils.

Stencil trees and houses

In advance of printing with Nursery Class, I prepared a handful of small stencils of invented trees and houses, on A4-sized tracing paper. These were drawn in pencil and cut with scissors. I kept both parts of each stencil – the tree- or house-shaped cut-out and the paper surround with its tree- or house-shaped hole. I attached the stencils with Blu-tack® to patterned gift wrap pieces and London A-Z map pages. Working with one child at a time (whilst another two or three worked, with minimal supervision, printing random pictures using DIY toy brick printers) I prepared a slab with green ink into which each child pressed a sponge printer. The child then dabbed the inked sponge all over the exposed areas of printing paper, making sure that ink was dabbed right up to the stencil's borders so that, when we peeled it off, the outline of the printed shape was crisp and clear. Although the stencils quickly became inky, it was possible, with care, to re-use each one several times during the session. Each stencil took only a minute or two to print.

Two Nursery Class children sponge printing a paper stencil of a house, in green ink, onto pink patterned gift wrap. The stencil was held in place with Blu-tack®; here it is starting to pull away from the printing paper

BELOW *Tree* and *House* paper stencil prints, sponge printed in green ink onto scraps of patterned pink gift wrap, by Nursery Class children

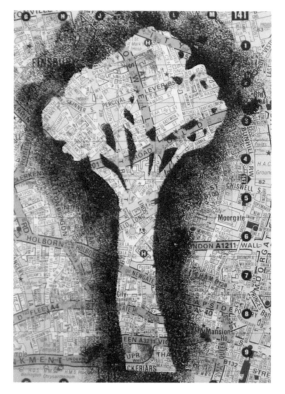

ABOVE LEFT AND RIGHT Stencil printed trees by Nursery Class children, printed in blue/black ink on London map pages. To print the tree on the left, the stencil was stuck down in the centre of the map page and sponge printed around its outline. When that print was complete, the inky stencil was peeled off and laid, ink side down, on the adjacent map page, with a thin, clean sheet of paper laid on top to keep the printing clean. A clean roller was used to roll the back of the clean sheet of paper, pressing through to the stencil, to transfer its wet ink to the map page and create the print on the right

RIGHT The same tree stencil printed by a Nursery Class child onto a brown paper, subtly patterned, gift wrap

Two Nursery Class children sponge printing paper stencils of (in the background and using two ink colours) a tree on pink patterned gift-wrap and (in the foreground) a house on a London map page. (The finished *House* print is shown on p.72)

BELOW Reception Class stencil prints, printed on transparent acetate sheets and paper, hung up to dry

Because stencils are fragile, you must work one-to-one with small children to stop them rubbing the inked sponges across the printing paper – this will rip or crease the stencil and spoil the print. To avoid this, you can print stencils without touching the paper by using a plant mister to spray liquid drawing ink or poster paint, or use two old toothbrushes – charge one with liquid ink and use the other to rub across the bristles of the first, spattering ink onto paper. These methods work but can be messy and results are variable. I find sponge-printing gives more consistent effects and is easier to control.

DIY stained glass

Prints on transparent acetate look like stained glass and can be displayed in windows to good effect. So, in advance of a printing session with Reception Class, I bought a stack of A4-sized sheets of transparent acetate – some colourless, some pale blue and yellow. I prepared simple tree-, house- and block of flats-stencils on tracing paper using, as previously, both the cut-out shape and paper surround. I prepared about 35 sheets of acetate (one per child plus spares), sticking a stencil in place with Blu-tack® on each sheet.

BELOW LEFT *Untitled* 'stained glass' print by Reception Class child. Paper stencil print on yellow acetate. The tree and house stencil was attached to the acetate with Blu-tack® and the area around it was first sponge-printed in red, then over-printed using a DIY brick printer textured with bubble-wrap

BELOW RIGHT An offset print rubbed from the wet 'stained glass' print onto white paper. The result is a paler, mirror-image variant of the print on acetate. The acetate print, however, being transparent, can be displayed to show the tree on the left or right as preferred

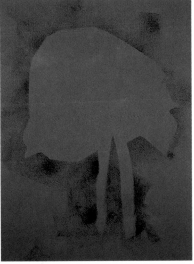

An offset print rubbed from a different wet 'stained glass' print onto white paper (Reception Class)

Sponge printing, in black ink on red paper, of a Reception Class child's own stencil, which he cut from thin card and printed

The 30 children were arranged six to a table, with a slab rolled with extended red ink for each group. Each child was given a sponge printer and a sheet of acetate (with attached stencil). They sponged red ink all over the acetate to define the stencil's outlines. Then the sponges were left to soak in a sink of warm, soapy water while the slabs were rolled with black ink, rolled straight over the remains of the red, using the same rollers without cleaning them first. (This was only possible because the second printing colour was much darker than the first. If it had been paler or a mid-tone, it would have been necessary to clean rollers and slabs between printings). The children used one DIY block printer each, with a particular, distinctive pattern, to print a layer of black on the acetate, on top of the red. Once done, adults peeled off the stencils. The red and black colours were selected because this classic colour combination has clarity and boldness – like Soviet Constructivist posters or Japanese lacquerwork – but any colours should work – the choice is yours! I extended the red ink significantly to render it translucent – so the sun would shine through like stained glass.

Because acetate is not absorbent, the ink sat, very wet, on its surface and was prone to smudging. To help the 'stained glass' dry and get more prints from the session, I had prepared a range of smooth white and coloured papers to the size of the acetate. I laid a piece in place to cover each printed sheet and the children then rolled the back of these papers with clean rollers (or I rubbed the back with my fist) to transfer excess wet ink from the acetate onto paper and thus gain a second print – a paler mirror-image of the first. In some cases, where the acetate was still very wet, we managed to pull a third print from it onto fresh paper. Acetate and printed papers were pegged up to dry – taking care that the acetates didn't rub against one another as the damp ink readily transfers from or sticks one sheet to another. They took about a week to dry, as opposed to a day or two for prints on paper. The whole project took a little under an hour and a half. To consolidate and extend what they had learned, the children then spent an hour creating their own stencils from thin card and printing them, using sponges and black ink, onto coloured paper.

River Thames panorama

This project for Year 2 was to create a panoramic view of the River Thames on 30 individual sheets of paper so that each child would have their own print while, at the same time, each print would comprise part of a larger panorama that would move from day to night as the image progressed. The teacher took her class sketching along the river, near Tate Modern, paying particular attention to the outline shapes of buildings against sky as we would later develop these drawings into paper stencils for printing.

1 Preparing the printing paper

Several days in advance, I cut some large pieces of white Somerset Satin (250 gsm) printing paper into 30 A4-size sheets. I chose this thick paper because my plan would involve repeated over-printing – so the paper needed the capacity to soak up many ink layers. I started preparations myself so that we could be sure to finish the project in the time available. I prepared, in my studio, an extremely pale, extended, blue ink and rolled this onto the first half dozen sheets of paper. These would be 'early morning' prints. Rolling the colour on was quick and not completely even – irregularities would be covered by later printing. I gradually increased the opacity of ink on slab (adding incrementally more colour and less extender) so that, as I rolled ink onto the next batch of paper, it became bluer – moving towards midday and afternoon tones. Having printed about 15 sheets, I began, gradually, to

House on a map by Nursery Class child. Stencil print, sponge-printed in blue/green ink on a London map page

introduce pink/purple hues, to suggest sunset and dusk, until, finally, in the last half dozen, I was rolling a deep purple/black night hue. On the first print, I stuck a small paper stencil in the top left so that, after rolling it with blue ink and peeling off the stencil, a white sun-like shape appeared in the 'day sky'. On the last sheet, I stuck a similar stencil in the top right corner and rolled ink over it so that, when it was peeled away, a white, round, moon-shape appeared in the 'night sky'. I pegged the sheets up to dry, keeping them in order of printing, and numbered them on the back, one to 30, palest to darkest.

2 Starting the stencils

Next day, I stuck an A4-sized tracing paper sheet on each of the 30 pieces of printing paper, fixing it with masking tape along one of its two shorter edges so that the tracing paper could be lifted and lowered, like opening a greetings card. Each child's riverscape was to take a horizontal format, with river and skyline in exactly the same place on each print. Eventually, they would hang side by side in an unbroken line to suggest one long river with buildings along its banks.

I wrote the word TOP along one long edge of the tracing paper (to define where the sky would be), then measured from that edge 13cm (almost two thirds of the way) down each of the two shorter sides and drew a pencil line across the tracing paper to link these two points. This line would demarcate where land would meet water. I drew a second line, parallel with the first, but about 1cm below it. This would mark the darkest area of shadow/reflection where buildings would meet water and would provide strong differentiation between land and river.

I cut along along each of these two lines with scissors. The tracing paper was now separated into three parts – the one marked TOP being the largest, then a thin strip only 1cm wide, then a strip about 7cm deep – but all parts remained attached, with masking tape along one side, to the printing paper. I repeated the whole process on the other 29 papers. With more time, I would have involved the class in these preparations as, apart from learning how to make stencils, it would have given them practice measuring and counting.

3 Organising the class

In the artroom, we set up six trestle tables to form three sides of a square (with my table for demonstrating techniques and stockpiling equipment along the fourth side). The children were arranged, five per table, along three outside edges of this square. (We didn't worry about chairs; it was easier to print standing up!) I distributed the printing papers with stencils attached, one per child, in the order in which I had printed them.

Pink Tree by Nursery Class child. Stencil print, sponge-printed in blue ink onto pink and white patterned gift wrap

4 Finishing the stencils

I asked the children to measure 7cm down from the TOP on each of the two shorter edges of their tracing paper and to mark those two points, joining the dots with a ruled pencil line (many needed help.) This line was to mark the approximate place on their prints where buildings would meet sky – but some tower blocks might be taller than this line and other low-rise structures would fall below it. (These stencil measurements were based on a balance of sky to buildings to river that I considered aesthetically pleasing – fairly arbitrary choices. For more sky and shorter buildings or a greater depth of river, simply change the measurements and thus the relative sizes of stencils to achieve a different balance.)

Using their riverbank sketches as inspiration, the children drew a pencil skyline across the tracing paper, starting and ending at the two pencil points they had just measured. Drawing a skyline involves making one continuous unbroken line – but a line that might move horizontally, then up and across and down to denote tower or chimney, or curve for a domed roof, or zigzag for triangular outlines of rooftops or church spires. No architectural details need be drawn. Many children were inclined to make their buildings' outlines too small and cramped – so the shapes would later be hard to cut with scissors. They needed encouragement to think bigger in their drawing.

Next, each child cut carefully along their undulating pencil line, thus dividing the large piece of tracing paper into two irregularly shaped pieces, each still attached to the printing paper by masking tape on one edge. Many needed help with this and to stick back, with masking tape, any larger bits of stencil they accidentally chopped off! This task, from drawing to finished cutting, took at least three quarters of an hour.

5 Printing buildings and their river reflections

All stencils were still attached by masking tape along one edge of the printing paper so, leaving only the stencil marked TOP in place, we lifted the buildings' stencil and the two strips of river stencils round to the back of the printing paper, out of the way. Adults prepared a dozen ink slabs – two per table. We used darker hues – blues and reds – for printing on the paler and mid-blue 'daytime' papers and increasingly light colours – opaque pinks, blues and yellows – for printing on the purple 'sunset', 'evening' and 'night' papers.

On spare paper prepared with the same stencils, I demonstrated how to print the buildings using DIY printers (see Chapter 6). The children shared blocks between them, taking turns to print particular textures, using a variety of printers on each print. They printed the blocks in vertical patterns or stripes, from top to bottom of the paper; the printing in the top section would come to resemble windows and

Printing with yellow ink the narrow strip dividing buildings from river

other architectural forms while (after subsequent printings) the lower sections would look like their reflections in water.

Many children achieved this well. Those that didn't, printing in a more random way, still achieved effects that suggested buildings – but ones that were leaning or collapsing! It was vital to have at least three adults to watch all 30 children and stop them if they seemed to be printing too many layers and thus potentially transforming an image with variegated textures and patterns into a muddy blob! This printing stage took only five or ten minutes, then we lifted the buildings' stencil and the lower portion of river stencil round from the back to cover the front again so that now the only part of the printing paper exposed was the narrow strip separating buildings from river.

6 Printing the river bank

Using the same ink and printers, the children printed with just one printer all over that exposed strip. (Those printing on 'daytime' papers printed with dark colours and those with 'evening' or 'night' papers used paler colours – as previously.) This created a clear division between buildings and water. The children printed randomly, not in orderly stripes, the intention being simply to cover that strip in a dense layer of colour; it was done in barely a minute. Now the wider stencil strip covering the rest of the 'river' was peeled up and wrapped around to the back so that the entire river area was now exposed.

By this point, the children had been working for an hour and were due a break. This interlude gave the adults time to rinse and pack away the DIY printers, clean the slabs and prepare them with

ABOVE LEFT Year 2 child cutting along the skyline he has drawn on tracing paper, to create a 'buildings' stencil for his part of the *River Thames panorama* print. Note the word 'Top' written along one edge of the tracing paper, to define where the sky will be in his print. You can also see the wide stencil strip covering the 'river' area of the planned print and the thin strip of stencil dividing buildings from river. The stencils are attached to the pale blue printing paper by masking tape along a short edge

ABOVE RIGHT Printing in blue ink, with a DIY toy brick printer (wound with string to created a ribbed/stripy texture), along the thin strip dividing buildings from river in a Year 2 child's *River Thames panorama* stencil print. This is the only area of printing paper exposed at this point. All other parts of the image are covered with (now very inky) paper stencils fresh colours: pale yellows for daytime prints, pinks for sunsets and creamy white for night. When the class returned, we had 45 minutes to finish the prints.

7 Printing river water

The next step was to create a texture suggesting river ripples. I had prepared 15 toy bricks with a surface of thin corrugated card (from an art shop's collage pack). Its texture was in undulating, wave-like zigzags. Printing them was so quick that the class didn't mind sharing – one block between two children – and watching each other's prints take shape. They printed these new blocks horizontally across the page, covering all the river area; the resulting printed texture looked

ABOVE Peeling back the lower two stencils (a thin paper strip and a wider one) to expose the river area of a *Thames panorama* print to be printed with a texture to suggest water ripples. All other parts of the print remain covered by stencils at this point. (The finished print is shown on facing page)

Year 2 *River Thames panorama* stencil prints, laid out, in sequence, in two strips. On the left is the daytime section; on the right are the early evening and nighttime sections with the moon clearly visible in the last one

convincingly like water ripples catching sun- or moonlight. Only a small amount of printing was needed so that the textures printed earlier would still be visible through the ripples. It was important that these blocks were printed horizontally or the effect of water would be lost. Also, the horizontal printing would have a unifying effect across all 30 prints, adding to their cohesion when displayed as a single vista.

This stage of printing took barely five minutes, then both stencil strips for the river were brought round from the back to cover the front (sticking to the fresh ink) and the stencil marked TOP was peeled back and tucked behind so that the only exposed area of printing paper was now the sky. The printing blocks were collected up for washing,

8 Printing the sky
Without cleaning the slabs, I added white ink to each one – happy for this to mix with the residue of pinks and yellows to create subtly tinted whites – and handed out clean sponge printers. Using one

River Thames panorama by Anne Desmet. Demonstration stencil print, printed in yellow, red and blue ink on (blue-inked) Somerset Satin paper, using sponges and variously textured DIY toy brick printers. This was printed in step-by-step stages during the lesson, to show the Year 2 class each stage of the process

LEFT Detail of six prints of Year 2's *River Thames panorama*. Daytime prints on pale blue printed paper are in the foreground and evening prints on purple printed paper behind

RIGHT *River Thames panorama* by the author's daughter Marion in Year 2. Paper stencil printed with sponges and variously textured DIY toy brick printers on dark blue (printed) Somerset Satin paper

LEFT *River Thames panorama* by Year 2 child. Paper stencil printed with sponges and variously textured DIY toy brick printers on pale blue (printed) Somerset Satin paper

RIGHT *River Thames panorama* by Year 2 child. Paper stencil printed with sponges and variously textured DIY toy brick printers on purple (printed) Somerset Satin paper. The building on the left side of this child's printed skyline is clearly recognisable as Cannon Street railway station, London

sponge printer per child, the class sponged lightly over the lower portion of sky – paying special attention to the irregular outline of the buildings' stencil. This would give those buildings strong, clear definition, add a subtle sky texture suggestive of clouds and the printed sky would gain a naturalistic two-tone effect where the newly sponged colour would overprint on the original sky tone, but leaving that base hue exposed at the top edge of the paper. This last stage took only a few minutes.

River Thames panorama by Year 2 child. Paper stencil printed with sponges and variously textured DIY toy brick printers on deep purple (printed) Somerset Satin paper. Tate Modern is visible in the top left of this skyline

9 Cleaning up and finishing off

The final job was to peel all stencils off every child's print. This needed care and clean hands so, before we began, some children were sent to wash their hands whilst others collected sponges, rollers and slabs and washed them (before they too washed their hands). Meanwhile the adults peeled off the stencils and arranged the prints in a line, end to end, so the children could see their full panoramic effect.

8 Plasticine and mixed-media prints

Plasticine (modelling dough) can be moulded and indented to make distinctive, unusual, printers.

1 Place it on a warm radiator for five or ten minutes to soften sufficiently for children to knead it.

2 Roll it into a large ball then flatten one surface by pressing the ball onto a table top.

3 Press into this flat surface bits and pieces such as dried pasta shapes, screws, buttons, keys, bottle-tops or paper-clips. These can be left shallowly embedded or carefully lifted out, leaving their impressions behind.

4 Stab the surface with fork or comb prongs, pen lids, Lego® bricks or use a pencil to make a drawing on it. Roll the edge of a ribbed jar-lid across it for striped patterns.

5 You can also mould Plasticine to make figure- or car-shapes perhaps – but make sure that one surface is flat enough to be printed.

6 Try not to make the shape too complex as small pieces will become detached in the printing.

7 Ink the Plasticine block by pressing it directly into wet ink or by gentle roller-inking. Oil-based water-washable Caligo™ ink works well whereas standard oil-based ink tends to lift away from Plasticine's waxy surface. Water-based ink is repelled by the waxy Plasticine; to remedy this, mix a drop of washing-up liquid into this ink before applying it to the block.

8 To print it, simply press by hand onto paper. Take care not to press the block too hard as its malleable surface quickly distorts.

Although you can get quite a few prints from a Plasticine block, they will all be different as the block distorts with every printing, but children enjoy making them and they can be surprisingly effective.

The Gherkin by Year 4 child. Plasticine, paper stencil, sponge and DIY textured printers on red Lhokta paper

81

A big red bus and a block of flats

Having worked on assorted individual prints with Reception Class, I thought it would be a positive challenge for this group to work together on a couple of very large pictures. Staying with the theme 'Our London' I drew out two large stencils of a London bus and a block of flats (with adjoining house) on tracing paper measured to fit large pieces of Somerset Satin (300 gsm) white printing paper. My stencils had, between them, at least 30 windows of similar shapes and sizes; so, before cutting them out, I made a quick sketch of the bus and flats, on which I gave each window a number. On each stencil I numbered the windows in the same sequence so that, once cut out, I would easily and accurately be able to reassemble them.

Then I cut out the outline shapes of the stencils as well as all windows and doors, being careful to keep every single piece including the tracing paper surround outside the bus (this would be needed to keep the printing paper clean, outside the image area). I laid out all the separate parts of the stencils – fitting them together like jigsaws – on the two sheets of printing paper. I stuck them down using tiny bits of rolled up masking tape (but Blu-tack® works better as masking tape is harder to peel off).

1 Organising the class

The class was divided into four groups of seven or eight. The groups would be rotated so each child would have a go at every task but, initially, one group would work on the bus, the next on the flats, while the third would make Plasticine printers of faces and the fourth would play with DIY printing blocks in an unstructured activity requiring minimal supervision. As each stage of stencil-printing on bus and flats was completed, groups were rotated so a different group each time added more to each large print and, in the end, every child had also made a Plasticine face and had a go at the unstructured activity.

The paper with the bus stencil was laid out across a trestle table, the flats stencil across another and a further two or three tables were placed end to end so that, at one end, children could work with adults to make DIY Plasticine blocks and, at the other end, could print DIY printers.

2 Plasticine faces

Having warmed the Plasticine while we prepared the room for printing, each group in turn made a 'face' printer by rolling a golf-ball-sized lump into a rough ball, then bashing one 'side' flat against a tabletop. I had brought a collection of bits and pieces (as described on p.81) that they could press into the Plasticine to make eyes, noses and mouths. As each model was completed, staff put it on a window ledge until it was needed.

Big red bus

1 The red of the bus

I peeled off the main section of the stencil – the bus shape – leaving everything else stuck down, namely all windows, doors, wheels, 'Lauriston' logo and edge surround. Seven children sponge-printed in red over the whole paper, making sure every bit was printed. Once done, the bus-shaped stencil was laid back in place to protect the red printing underneath; it stuck well to the freshly-printed ink.

2 Wheels and doors

Now, the round wheel stencils were lifted off, leaving every other stencil in place. The exposed printing paper was sponge-printed black and the wheel stencils laid back in place, sticking to the fresh ink. Now the stencils covering the lower halves of each door were lifted off and the exposed paper sponge-printed blue. We didn't bother putting door stencils back before moving on to the final stage.

3 Passengers on the bus

I peeled off every window stencil plus the top halves of doors, leaving all other stencils in place. With pink ink rolled on one slab and brown on another, about half the class, one at a time, pressed their Plasticine face into their preferred colour and we pressed each face into a different window. When every one was printed, the remaining stencils were peeled away to reveal the finished print.

ABOVE LEFT Reception Class children sponge printing the first stage of their large London bus print. The printing paper is exposed only in the areas to be printed red. All other parts – windows, doors, wheels and lettering – are protected by paper stencils

ABOVE RIGHT Once the first stage of printing was complete, the stencil showing the bus's framework was laid back in place to protect the printing underneath it, while the 'wheel' stencils were peeled away so the exposed areas could be sponge printed black. (At this stage, all other parts of the printing paper were covered by paper stencils – some now covered in red ink from the first stage of printing)

ABOVE Printing Plasticine faces in the bus's windows. At this point, the doors have also been sponge printed (in blue ink) and the stencils protecting the windows peeled away

ABOVE Peeling off the last bits of stencil (around the bus's wheel rims) to reveal the finished print

BELOW *Lauriston bus* by Reception Class. Paper stencil and Plasticine block prints on Somerset Satin paper, 56.5x76cm

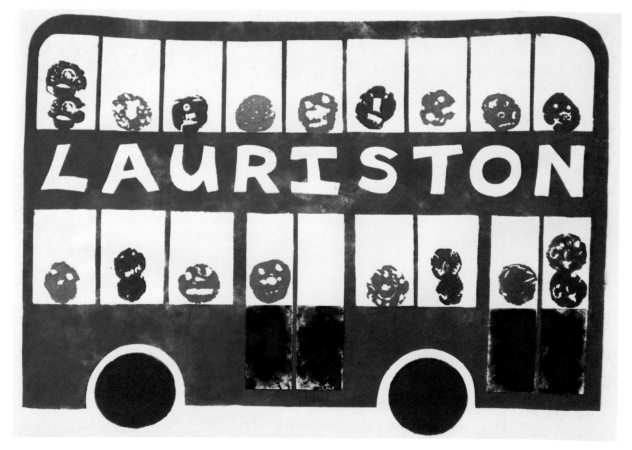

Block of flats

1 Blue walls

I began by carefully peeling off the main section of the stencil – the shape of the flats with adjoining house – leaving everything else stuck down – windows, doors, sky and moon stencils. Using two or three inked slabs, eight children sponge-printed blue over the whole paper, making sure every exposed bit was printed. Then the main section of stencil was laid back in place to protect the blue printing underneath.

2 Night sky and door knobs

Stencils covering the two door knobs as well as that covering the sky area were lifted off and the exposed printing paper sponge-printed black. We replaced the door knob stencils before moving to the next stage.

3 Red doors

Now the rectangular door stencils were lifted off, leaving every other stencil in place. The exposed paper was sponge-printed red. We didn't bother replacing these stencils before moving to the next stage.

4 Faces at the windows

I peeled off every window stencil leaving all others in place. Using pink or brown ink, each child (who had not already printed a face on the bus) inked their Plasticine face and we pressed each one into a different window of the flats. When every one was printed, the remaining stencils, including the round, unprinted moon were peeled off to reveal the finished print.

BELOW LEFT Reception Class children sponge printing the first stage of their large *Block of flats* print. The printing paper is exposed only in areas to be printed blue. All other parts – windows, doors, moon and sky – are protected by paper stencils

BELOW RIGHT The stencil showing the framework of the flats has been laid back in place to protect the blue printing underneath it, while the night sky and door handles have now been printed black. The stencils for the handles have been laid back in place to stop the freshly-printed black ink muddying the next colour to be printed. Window stencils are still in place but are covered in blue ink from the first stage of printing. Now the door stencils have been peeled away so the exposed areas can be sponge-printed red

Rolling out pink and brown inks to print the Plasticine faces at the windows of the flats, after the red printing of the doors is complete

The same colours: red, blue, black, pink and brown were used for both large prints so that, rather than having to prepare fresh ink slabs at each stage, the same few slabs with these colours could be rotated between both activities to limit the washing up later. The teacher kept the unwashed Plasticine faces for a classroom display and to print on Easter baskets later.

Printing the Plasticine faces with simple hand pressure

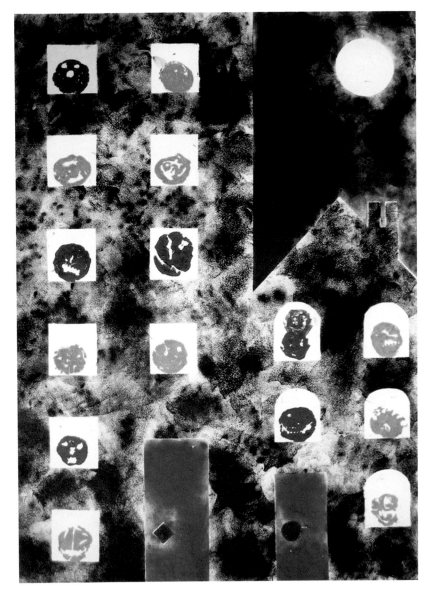

Block of flats by Reception Class. Paper stencil and Plasticine block prints on Somerset Satin paper, 76x56.5cm. No colour was used to print the moon. The round stencil was simply peeled away at the end to expose the clean white paper beneath it

BELOW *Night sky* by Year 5. Large stencil print, printed in cream and green inks on black sugar paper, using sponges and DIY printers. Like Reception Class's *Block of Flats* print, this was a larger-scale project involving children printing simultaneously on the same image using assorted mixed-media printers

Canary Wharf and the Gherkin

By Year 4, many children's drawings tend to be influenced by Disney or Japanese Manga cartoons. While there's nothing wrong with this, it doesn't necessarily widen their perceptions of different ways of drawing. With this in mind, I decided to challenge this group to manipulate Plasticine into printable models.

1 Plasticine buildings: making and printing

The children first rolled their Plasticine into ovoid shapes (for London's Gherkin building) or cuboids for Canary Wharf tower, using preparatory sketches and photos for reference. As Canary Wharf is so tall, I suggested making a textured cube-shaped block that could be printed two or three times in a vertical sequence, one printing lining up exactly with the next to create a single, tall, tower-image, with a separate triangular-shaped block to print the roof. Several children found this approach easier than trying to manipulate one larger Plasticine model. Plasticine is easiest to manage in child's fist-sized or smaller lumps.

Next, they indented their blocks, shallowly, with ridged objects including dried pasta fusilli, Lego® bricks, toy car tyre treads, the textured pattern on the belly of a rubber snake and some flower-shaped plastic beads. These textures – especially the Lego® – effectively suggested architectural details such as round windows.

When the blocks were complete (which took about three quarters of an hour), we printed them all in deep blue ink (for speed and ease of cleaning as we only needed one roller to prepare half a dozen slabs) onto white and coloured Japanese and Nepalese artists' papers (torn down, in advance, to roughly A4-size). This occupied a full 90-minute session.

2 Beginning the stencils

With this project, I had not developed a clear plan because I wasn't sure how the Plasticine prints would turn out – so I wanted to keep my options open. Looking through the prints (once dry), I felt that the Plasticine's indented textures had printed successfully but, in many cases, the outline shapes of buildings needed stronger definition and the towers all appeared to float in the middle of each sheet – they needed a foreground and background. I decided stencilling would be useful. I hinged A4 tracing paper (with masking tape) to the top edge of each child's print so that the tracing paper lay over the front of the printed image, its edges lined up with those of the printing paper. I drew a simple pencil tracing around each ovoid or rectangular printed tower – defining more clearly the characteristic shapes of the Gherkin and Canary Wharf. This job,

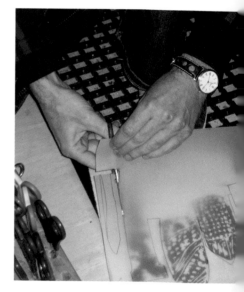

Cutting a paper stencil more clearly to define the architectural structure in a Year 4 Plasticine block print that can be seen underneath the tracing paper. (The outline for the stencil should, ideally, be a continuous, unbroken line defining the skyline. This stencil shows a few extra, unnecessary lines)

repeated for each child's print, took an hour or two. (I did this preparation to ensure the class would have time to finish and print their stencils in their one remaining session. With more time, they could have done this job themselves.)

3 Finishing the stencils

In the next session, we began by completing the stencils. I asked the children to look at the traced lines I had started and continue drawing to the left and right of those outlines – linking up with my drawing at both sides to add the contours of additional real or invented buildings in a skyline extending across the page. Once done, we cut along the drawn line, right across the tracing paper, ending with two stencil pieces on each print – the top stencil (covering what would be sky) still attached by tape hinges to the printing paper and the stencil from the lower half now completely detached. Each child wrote his/her name on the detached part before they were collected and put away. This all took about an hour.

A washing line of prints from Plasticine blocks, made by Year 4, printed in blue ink on red and yellow Nepalese Lhokta papers and off-white Japanese Kozu-shi paper. The Plasticine block used to create the print of Canary Wharf tower (on red paper) clearly shows the impressions of Lego® toy bricks used to indent the Plasticine. These prints are unfinished, awaiting later printing with stencils and assorted DIY printers

4 Printing the foreground

With the top stencils in place, the children printed all over the exposed area of printing paper (but avoided printing, as far as possible, on top of the Plasticine-printed towers) using assorted DIY toy brick printers (described in Chapter 6) and plenty of colours – orange, red, green, pink, brown and purple – that adults mixed and rolled onto about a dozen inking slabs (two for each colour). The DIY blocks had various textured materials attached, including: bubble wrap, corrugated card, elastic bands, indented polystyrene, part of a crocheted-string doily and furry pipe cleaners. I asked the children to print these blocks up the paper, vertically, or across it, horizontally, so that the printed patterns and overlapping colours would create impressions of layers of new buildings. I had also prepared DIY blocks to which I had stuck bits of flat collage-foam cut into simple house shapes. These could be printed as 'stand alone' buildings or incorporated into an overall effect with other printers. Finally, I had sliced half a dozen broccoli florets in half. Printing their flat, cut surfaces produced convincing trees. To keep the colours on each slab clean, I laid out a selection of blocks with each slab, so the children used different blocks for different colours, rather than inking the same block in different colours. When this printing stage was complete (it took about half an hour), we peeled off the stencils. At this stage many prints, while vividly coloured and full of textures, still lacked compositional clarity, which would be provided by printing the second stencil.

5 Printing the background

The lower sections of the stencils were retrieved and distributed. Each child laid their second stencil in place, sticking it to the wet ink to cover, as precisely as possible, all printing so far undertaken. With fresh ink slabs rolled in pale blue, cream and pale pink, the children printed the exposed sky of their prints using toy trucks 'driven' through the wet ink to ink up their textured tyres and then 'driven' in parallel lines to make 'mackerel sky' effects or, more randomly, to suggest rays of sunshine. Alternatively or additionally children used sponge printers to create an overall sky tone – taking care to print right up to the irregular edge of the stencil so that all buildings' outlines would achieve optimum clarity. We also printed sea sponges to suggest clouds. When this was done (barely 15 minutes), stencils were peeled away to reveal the finished prints.

The finished *Canary Wharf tower* print on red Lhokta paper (shown, after its first stage of printing, on p.89). Photo © Madeleine Waller 2008

ABOVE LEFT Additional buildings printed by Year 4 children on papers previously printed with their Plasticine block printers. The stencil of the foreground print has been peeled back to show the progress of printing (with textured DIY toy brick printers) at this stage

ABOVE RIGHT Print in progress showing Plasticine- and DIY-block-printed buildings. The sky has yet to be printed (see right), which will more clearly define the architecture

LEFT Year 4 child holding her finished print. Printed on off-white, Japanese, Kozu-shi paper, the blue printed tree and foreground tower are printed with Plasticine blocks; the background (purple) skyline is created with a paper stencil printed with DIY, textured, toy-brick printers; the green trees in the foreground are printed broccoli florets; the green house is printed from a cut foam shape glued to a toy wooden brick; the border of green semi-circles is simply the printed end of a shaped toy brick

RIGHT *Canary Wharf tower* by Year 4 child. The final stage of printing involved masking off the printed buildings with another stencil and printing a textured sky by running a toy truck through wet cream-coloured ink then 'driving' it, in parallel lines, up the red printing paper. Photo © Madeleine Waller 2008

ABOVE *Canary Wharf skyline* by Year 4 child. Plasticine, paper stencil, sponge and DIY textured printers on Japanese Kozu-shi paper. Dark blue elements are printed from Plasticine blocks; the green tree is printed broccoli; textured buildings are printed using assorted DIY toy-brick printers; and blue sky is sponge-printed around a paper stencil

LEFT *Skyline with Gherkin and Canary Wharf* by Year 4 child. Plasticine, paper stencil, sponge and DIY textured printers on yellow Lhokta paper. Dark blue elements are printed from Plasticine blocks and the mauve 'lacy' texture is from a shop-bought rubber stamp printer

RIGHT *Canary Wharf skyline* by Year 4 child. Plasticine, paper stencil, sponge and assorted DIY textured printers on Japanese Kozu-shi paper. Photo © Madeleine Waller 2008

9 Mixed-media collage prints (collagraphs)

Printing plates that are in themselves beautiful, sculptural artworks can be made from thin card and other relatively flat objects glued to a stiff card or mountboard base. Prints made this way are called collagraphs.

1 Consider what textures and patterns you would like in your print:
   a corrugated card prints stripes;
   b sandpaper prints speckled textures;
   c cereal box card can be cut into shapes and indented with a pencil or biro design;
   d bubble-wrap prints with a distinctive spot-pattern;
   e fabric (and paper) doilies, string, netting, leaves and lace print their own designs;
   f crumpled paper or tin-foil provide interestingly random textures;
   g furry pipe cleaners print as thick, fuzzy-edged lines;
   h paper clips, mirror plates (for fixing framed pictures to walls), keys and coins print with their own characteristics.

2 Make sure all collage components are of similar height as too much variation will make them hard to ink and print. If, for instance, a piece of netting is much shallower than adjacent materials, stick it to a piece of card to increase its height before pasting it to the base.

3 Thin card can be cut into shapes, hole-punched and indented with drawings in biro or hard pencil.

4 Make sure everything is firmly glued in place.

5 For best durability, use PVA glue and leave overnight to dry.

6 Seal the block's surface by painting on a dilute layer of PVA. The block will then withstand many printings (and can also be printed using water-based inks, which will quickly turn an unsealed block soggy and useless).

7 Alternatively, for a more instant but less durable block, most components can be glued with a non-toxic, water-washable glue stick, but be sure to use double-sided tape for foil, bubble-wrap and any other items that don't glue well.

8 Don't worry about sealing the block if you don't intend to take more than about six prints from it.

9 Print it (once glue has dried) with regular oil-based or oil-based water-washable ink.

10 Collage blocks can be roller-inked, but localised inking with a dabber is useful for areas the roller may miss or to apply extra colours.

11 Lay a sheet of paper over the block and print by roller or spoon-burnishing.

12 Leave ink to dry on the block after printing (which will, to an extent, seal it and enable you to print from it again another day); or leave it to dry and keep the block (as well as prints!) for display.

ABOVE LEFT Year 1 children glueing thin cardboard collage pieces to thicker card base plates

ABOVE RIGHT A finished collagraph plate made with bubble wrap, cereal box and corrugated card. The overlapping of some collaged pieces makes this example harder to print than plates with no overlapping elements

Collaged street scenes

1 Gathering materials

Before a lesson with Year 1 I obtained, for free from a picture framer's shop, small offcuts of picture mountboard. (Most picture framers have lots of such offcuts that usually get thrown away. Using them for collagraphs recycles them.) None of these rectangular or square pieces was larger than 20cm²; they were a perfect, manageable size and

ABOVE Freshly inked Year 1 collagraph plate comprising indented, cut and torn cereal box and corrugated card, bubble wrap, lace, netting and paper clip

LEFT *Street scene* by Year 1 child. Collagraph print (from the plate shown above) in black, red and blue ink on white Japanese paper

Walking down the street by Year 1 child. Collagraph print in black, red and blue ink on white Japanese paper. Photo © Madeleine Waller 2008

thickness to make collagraph base plates. I collected up assorted collage materials (as described on p.96) but for ease of construction and printing, I pre-selected bits already of a consistent height and cut card, fabric and bubble-wrap into small rectangular, square, triangular and semi-circular shapes. I also cut large sheets of white, semi-transparent, Japanese printing paper into 60 or 70 sheets of about A4 size.

2 Making the plates

In the lesson, each child was given a base plate and pencil (to write their name on their plate). Each table (at which sat five or six children) was set with small bowls full of the collage materials. I asked the children to decide which edge of the base plate was to be the bottom of their picture and arrange materials along that edge as if they were creating a street. I asked them to consider the bowls' contents as components of houses, offices, shops and towers and to assemble them, however they liked, to look as much like buildings as possible, glueing their pieces with a glue stick.

A selection of Year 1's collagraph plates, after printing

BELOW *Houses* by Year 1 child. Collagraph print in black and red ink on Japanese paper

The only rules were :

a pieces of collage should not overlap as this would make some parts much thicker/higher than others, making them hard to print;

b collage should not stick out over the edge of the base plate as, again, this would make it hard to print; and

c the children should first compose their pictures by arranging their collage pieces on the base plate, before glueing anything down.

It took about three quarters of an hour for the class to complete this. Some hole-punched card and one or two used scissors to customise card shapes. When everyone's collage was glued down (children needed help with this), to finish each plate and personalise it, each child was given a biro or hard pencil with which to make an indented drawing on selected areas – which would show up clearly in the printing. They drew windows, doors and tiny figures on their collaged tower blocks and houses. (Some also drew on exposed areas of base plate but, since only the raised areas of collage can be easily inked and printed, any drawing here was unlikely to print.)

3 Printing the plates

Before the next lesson, I checked all the plates' components and re-glued any parts that weren't firmly stuck down. To gain strong graphic clarity, with the children's assistance, I inked and printed their blocks in black ink. Any areas the roller missed, we inked with a fabric dabber in red or blue, to add interest. When the block was inked, a sheet of the thin Japanese paper was laid onto it and printed by clean roller plus finger-tip pressure to burnish small areas the roller missed. An advantage of this semi-transparent paper was that the print showed through the back, making it entirely clear which areas needed extra burnishing. I printed two prints from each plate. The printing of all 30, twice over, took about an hour (hard going at one print every minute!) so, while I was printing with one child at a time, the rest of the class undertook a drawing activity.

Kite flying on Parliament Hill

Having made polystyrene prints with Year 3 based on their drawings of a kite-flying outing to London's Parliament Hill, I thought it would be interesting to treat the same subject in a different way, using collagraph combined with stencilling. This class had completed their polystyrene prints in about an hour and a half, leaving an hour that we used to make collage blocks.

1 Making the plates

In advance I tore sheets of Nepalese Lhokta paper in red and petrol blue hues to roughly A4-size (US: A-size) and cut 30 base plates to the paper size. I also made a collection of cereal and other food boxes, plus corrugated papers and cards. As these children were older, I did not pre-cut the cardboard but gave each child a pencil and scissors with which to design and cut their own shapes of hills, houses and kites – although they also used pre-cut pieces from Year 1's collage-making. The class was asked to create and glue a scene, in non-overlapping cardboard shapes, onto their blocks. They just managed this within the hour. I also asked each child to write their name on their block and on a sheet of the Lhokta printing paper (using the colour of their choice).

Year 3 child with her watercolour and pencil studies of classmates flying kites on Parliament Hill. Useful preparatory work made on a trip in advance of the printing session

2 Making stencils

Before the next session, I took the children's blocks home (to re-glue loose bits) as well as their (as yet unprinted) coloured papers. I began to prepare stencils, which were intended to create a skyline of houses in the background of each picture. Using A4 tracing paper, I hinged a sheet with masking tape to the top edge of each block. I considered each block in turn and thought about where a skyline might go. For instance, if a collage had a straight line of buildings along the bottom edge, then I drew a roughly horizontal line on the tracing paper, sometimes about a third of the way up, sometimes two thirds and sometimes not quite as high as the tallest buildings (working by instinct rather than by any fixed rules). If the child's collage followed a curve (as many children had cut rounded hill shapes out of which their buildings 'grew'), then I drew a similar curving line so that background would relate well to foreground. After each stencil line was drawn, I unstuck the tracing paper from each block and hinged it, instead, to the top edge of each child's named sheet of printing paper.

Kite flying on Parliament Hill by Year 3 child. Collagraph and stencil print in cream, red and black inks on blue-green Nepalese Lhokta paper

RIGHT *Kite flying on Parliament Hill* by Year 3 child. Collagraph and stencil print in cream, red and black inks on blue-green Nepalese Lhokta paper. Photo © Madeleine Waller 2008

In class, I asked the children to consider what I had drawn as the skyline for their print and treat it as the 'ground' on which they should now draw outlines of buildings and trees (that they might see from Parliament Hill) in a horizon line extending across the page. With scissors, we cut along these outlines, right across the tracing paper (taking care not to cut the printing paper), ending up with two stencil pieces for each block – the top piece still attached by tape hinges to the printing paper and the bottom piece now detached. We re-attached each bottom stencil with masking tape hinges along the bottom edge of each sheet of printing paper, ensuring it aligned accurately with the top stencil. This all took at least 45 minutes.

Aeroplane over Parliament Hill by Year 3 child. Collagraph and stencil print in cream, red and black inks on blue/green Nepalese Lhokta paper

3 Printing the background

Each child now carefully lifted the lower stencil out of the way by folding it around to lie flat at the back of the printing paper (while still securely attached to it by masking tape hinges). This left the upper stencil in place and the lower portion of the printing paper

RIGHT Year 3's collagraph plates after printing (with one unprinted example in the bottom left-hand corner)

revealed. I prepared about half a dozen ink slabs rolled with red ink. The children now spent 15 minutes printing all over the exposed part of the paper using DIY toy brick printers (described in Chapter 6), using their textures to create impressions of layers of buildings.

4 Printing the sky

The lower stencil was now pulled back to the front and laid in place (sticking to the wet ink) to cover all the printing just done, while the upper stencil was peeled off and discarded. With fresh slabs rolled with cream ink (white with a dash of yellow), the children now used sponge printers to print the exposed sky area of their prints to create an overall pale tone; they took care to print right up to and overlap the irregular edges of the stencil so that all the buildings' outlines would achieve optimum clarity. When complete (it took only about ten minutes), the stencils were peeled away.

5 Printing the collage plates

Because collage blocks are fragile – especially those not sealed with varnish – I roller-inked them myself. For this I used just one slab of black ink, topping it up with fresh ink after every three or four printings (I chose black ink to strengthen the impact of the printed collages and to clearly differentiate foreground from background). The printing paper was laid, face down, on top of the inked block (aligning both their bottom edges) and printed by roller. Printing all 30 plates took about an hour, so, while one child at a time printed with my supervision, the rest of the class printed the 'gift-wrap' illustrated in Chapter 6 and also a stencilled skyline print.

Trees and houses by Year 3 child. Collagraph and stencil print in cream, red and black inks on blue-green Nepalese Lhokta paper

10 *Multi-colour prints from cereal boxes*

Simple pieces of cereal or pizza box card can be turned into versatile printing blocks and several can be created and printed, one after another, on the same piece of paper, to create a multi-coloured print. For different effects try the following:

1 Cut or tear card to produce strong graphic forms or softer more textured printed effects.

2 Fold or crumple it, then smooth it out – crease-marks print as delicate thread-lines.

3 Draw with ballpoint pen or hard pencil: the indented picture prints.

4 Try inking different cardboard shapes in different colours, then assemble them, jigsaw-like, to print a multi-coloured image.

5 If printed with oil-based water-washable ink (or regular oil-based ink), cardboard blocks with a glazed (slightly shiny) surface will withstand five or six printings. If sealed first with PVA (as described for collagraphs in Chapter 9) they will last longer.

China town two-block prints

1 Advance preparations for a Year 2 lesson

I obtained (free from a picture framer) small offcuts of mountboard to use as base plates for collaged cereal box blocks. Because I planned to make prints involving two blocks per image, it was important to ensure that these plates were all the same size so that, when inked and printed, the colours would fall in neat alignment (or registration) within the same pre-determined outline. I trimmed 62 pieces of mountcard to exact A5-size (210x148mm/8.3x5.8in.) rectangles – two per child and two for me to create a demonstration two-block print. I had been saving up old cereal and pizza boxes and cut these into about 80 A5-size pieces – two per child, two for my demonstration print and the rest (plus smaller offcuts) in case anyone's collage went wrong and they wanted fresh card. Then I tore large sheets of white Somerset Satin 250gsm printing paper into 75 pieces of A4 size (297x210mm/ 11.7x8.3in.) to allow for two finished prints per child and a few spares. I chose this paper as it is strong enough to withstand several layers of ink. I then prepared my demonstration print.

Cereal box card (background) plate and freshly pulled print

Year 2 child's sketches of London's China Town (including pencil rubbings of Chinese characters on Soho's Chinese Gate). The class's preparatory drawings and photos were used as reference material both for this lesson and for an earlier session of polystyrene block printing

2 Making the background plates

At the start of the lesson, to help the children understand what we were trying to achieve, I showed them my demonstration print and the two cardboard blocks from which it had been printed. Then each child was given one base plate, one piece of A5 cereal box card, a pencil, scissors and a glue stick. I asked them to decide which edge of the base plate would be the bottom edge in their picture (it could take a horizontal or vertical format) and to lay the cereal packet card on top, in the same alignment. They then drew on the cereal box card a skyline that would be the backdrop for a China Town composition. Using their selected bottom edge as 'ground level', they drew houses with pointed or castellated roofs, office blocks, church spires and domes, all inspired by sketches and photographs of China Town (that they had used earlier to make polystyrene prints – see Chapter 5). With scissors, they cut the 'sky' away from the skyline and glued what was left of their cereal box card (the buildings) onto their base plates, shiny/printed side up, using plenty of gluestick and lining up the bottom edge of the cereal box card with the bottom edge of the base plate. Once the cereal card was glued in place, each child drew windows and doors on their buildings

Year 2 children with 'background' cardboard plates assembled and ready for printing. The plates held up by the two boys in the foreground are made from pieces of an old pizza box. The brand logo on the box was slightly raised and produced a distinctive, interesting pattern in the prints

using biros to indent the card. This all took about an hour and several children needed help cutting and sticking.

3 Printing the first plates

The children wanted a choice of colours so I rolled up one ink slab with a blue/green blend and another with a pink/purple one. Two adults then worked one-to-one with pairs of children to help them roller-ink their plates in their preferred colour options. The plates were easy to ink but, to maintain each blend, we needed to roll both slab and block in the same direction every time. A sheet of the Somerset Satin paper was laid onto the inked block and roller-printed with a clean roller. The prints were pegged up to dry. We printed two prints from each plate – with more time, we would have printed more, but two was the bare minimum to allow a margin for error when it came to over-printing the second plate. Two adults printing all 30 plates, twice over, took roughly an hour. While we were printing with two children at a time, the rest of the class had a 20-minute break and then, with three adult helpers, made their second printing plates.

4 Making the foreground plates

Each child was given a second base plate (and another piece of A5 cereal box card) and was asked to mark the bottom edge of this plate too, making sure it took the same vertical or horizontal format as the first. I asked the class to draw the outline shape (or shapes) on this cereal packet card of an image they would like in the foreground of their picture. Several drew Chinese dragons, some drew cars, buses, trees, the Chinese Gate and houses. They then glued these small shapes (shiny side up) to the second base plate, taking care to remember that the bottom edge of the base plate was the picture's bottom edge and so position the collage appropriately. Buildings and trees had to 'grow up' from the bottom whereas dragons, for instance, could be 'flying' higher up the picture plane. The only rules (as for collagraphs in Chapter 9) were:

a collage pieces should not overlap;

b collage should not stick out over the edges of the base plate; and

c children should compose the whole collage before glueing it down.

Pizza box print (in purple/pink ink blend on white Somerset Satin paper) printed from a plate made from an old pizza box (shown on previous and facing pages). The box's own raised pattern printed clearly, while the windows in the image were made by indenting the card with a hard pencil or ballpoint pen prior to inking and printing

RIGHT Year 2's cereal and pizza box 'background' plates, after inking and printing

ABOVE Year 2 child's cut-out cardboard 'beast/machine' about to be glued to a base card to create a foreground plate

LEFT Making a second cereal box printing plate to create an extra layer of imagery and colour in the finished print

It took about an hour for the entire class to complete their second plate but, as printing their first plates was finished half an hour or so before the whole class finished the second one, I moved straight on to print the second blocks with children who had finished, while the rest caught up.

5 Printing the second plates

I decided these plates should be printed in a colour that would stand out clearly against the background. The children wanted a choice so I rolled up one slab in black, another in red. The teacher and I continued working one-to-one with pairs of children. Each child brought their second plate to the inking table plus the two prints from their first plate. The second block was inked; the first print was laid printing-side-up on a clean worktop. The newly-inked block was placed face down on it, lining up the blocks's edges exactly with the edges of the printed image, and the block was pressed firmly by hand so the wet ink would stick it to the paper. Block and paper were then turned over so that the paper was uppermost; it was then roller printed. This process was repeated for each child's second print, re-inking each of the 30 blocks between printings. It took us about an hour to complete 60 prints, during which time the rest of the class was occupied either finishing their second plates or cleaning up slabs and rollers we had used to print the first plates.

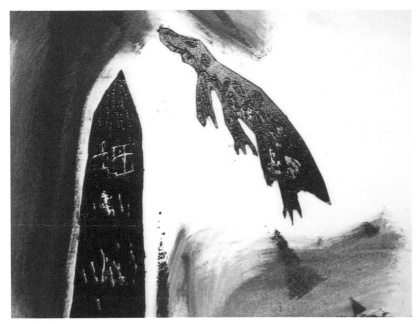

A Year 2 child's finished 'foreground' plate showing a collaged cardboard tower and dragon. This has been inked in black, ready for printing. Where the inked roller has caught the edges of the base plate, the ink was wiped off with a rag, prior to printing. The base plate makes a striking artwork in itself

BELOW *Dragon in China Town* by Year 2 child. Two-plate cereal box card print on white Somerset Satin paper. The background plate was inked in a green/blue blend; the foreground plate (see left) was inked in black. Photo © Madeleine Waller 2008

ABOVE *Houses in China Town* by Year 2 child. Two-plate cereal box card print on white Somerset Satin paper. The background plate was inked in a pink/purple blend; the foreground plate was inked in red. The raised, commercially printed lettering on the cereal box card of the background plate has added texture and interest to this print

LEFT A Year 2 child's finished 'foreground' plate showing a collaged cardboard dragon. This has been inked in red, ready for printing (see printed image, right)

RIGHT *Dragon in China Town* by Year 2 child. Two-plate cereal box card print on white Somerset Satin paper. The background plate was inked in a pink/purple blend; the foreground plate was inked in red. Excess red ink deposited by the roller along the edges of the second base plate was not wiped away prior to printing, so it has affected the final result. Also, this child's background plate took a vertical format while their foreground plate was horizontal. Printing is easier, with more consistent results, if both plates take the same alignment, but this is still a striking print

11 Linocuts

Linocuts are made from linoleum, a flooring material developed in the 1860s. Blocks will withstand dozens of printings. Lino is available in art materials' shops in small pre-cut rectangles, large sheets or very large rolls. Lino prints have a recognisable graphic character and their tradition in printmaking, stretching back to their use by Austrian schoolchildren in the early 1900s, is impressive.

Linocutting tools with detachable blades are cheap and widely available. However, they blunt quickly, are hard to sharpen and are difficult to use effectively – especially for children. I made linocuts with Years 5 and 6 and the children, without exception, found cutting much easier using artists' quality V and U gouges (with fixed blades), available from specialist suppliers, rather than any cheaper alternatives. 30 tools of artist's quality would be a significant expense for any school or individual artist (assuming 15 each of medium size V and U gouges for a class of 30 who could swap tools between them

BELOW LEFT A Year 6 child cutting a lino block. He is correctly keeping his free hand well clear of the path of the sharp metal gouge. He is cutting along the lines of a pencil drawing he made on the block

BELOW RIGHT *St Paul's Cathedral* by Year 6 child. Linocut print in yellow/blue-black ink blend on purple Canford paper

116

for access to both types) but, for sustained use, it might be a worthwhile investment preferable to constantly replacing cheap tools.

Preparation of lino

When you buy lino, its texture is slightly rough. Ideally, before cutting:

1 Place the block onto old newspapers (to soak up the mess) and pour about a tablespoon of water onto its surface.

2 Rub the surface all over with wet-and-dry sandpaper, through the water, adding more water as necessary. Even large blocks only take minutes to sand.

3 Wash the watery residue off with clean water and rags and leave to dry. The block's surface will now be much smoother and will print a more solid colour.

4 If the lino is too hard to cut easily, warm it with a hairdryer or by placing it on a radiator for a few minutes immediately before use.

Hackney Library by Year 5 child. Linocut and stencil print on blue Canford paper. The block was printed first in yellow ink; then it was cleaned and re-inked in red. Parts of the inked block were masked out with a tracing paper stencil before it was printed on top of the first printing, resulting in a two-colour print. Note that because the artist did not engrave the word 'Library' in reverse on her block, it has printed back-to-front in the top left corner of the print.
Photo © Madeleine Waller 2008

LEFT *Victoria Park bandstand* by Thomas, Year 5. Linocut print in cream-coloured ink on blue Canford paper

BELOW The lino block has been cleaned and re-inked in red. Tracing paper stencils are used to mask out portions of it. The red ink will only print in areas of the image that are not masked out

Preparatory drawing

1 Draw on lino with soft pencil.

2 Fix the drawing with permanent marker or felt-tip pen so it doesn't smudge while you are cutting.

3 Alternatively, work out the drawing on paper first, then copy or trace it on the block (remembering that the printed image will be a mirror image of your cutting, so reverse any lettering).

4 Since cut lines are likely to be two or three times broader than pencil-drawn ones, it helps to make a preparatory drawing, to scale, using broad-tippped marker pens. This gives a more accurate idea of the level of detail a child might accomplish.

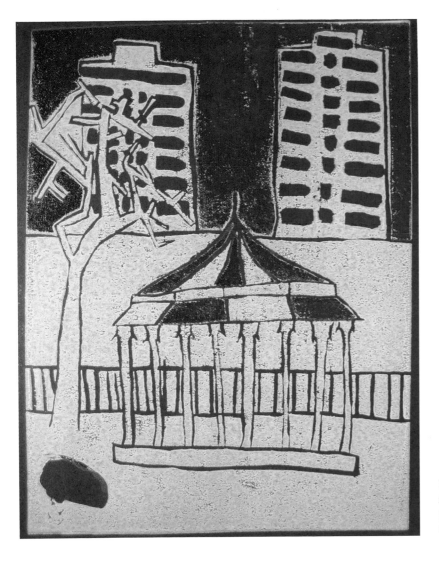

Victoria Park bandstand by the author's son, Thomas, Year 5. Linocut and stencil print in cream and red inks on blue Canford paper

Cutting the block

Everything you cut will be the white areas of the print (assuming printing is on white paper) as ink is applied to the block's uncut surface.

1 Use V-gouges for fine lines and U-gouges for thicker lines, for dots and for clearing away large areas.
2 To make a cut, hold the tool's handle in the palm of your hand, blade protruding between thumb and forefinger, then push the cutting edge into the lino, keeping hand and tool as flat against the block as you can.
3 Always cut away from your body and keep your free hand clear of the blade's path.

Printing in colour

You can print an image of many colours from just one block. In the reduction method, between printing each new colour, you continue cutting the same block, which gradually reduces its uncut surface. With this method, it is not possible later to reprint what you had earlier, so, to ensure a reasonable end quantity of successful prints, print plenty of extras at the beginning to allow for some mistakes with colour or registration in later printings. Alternatively, the multiple-block method requires a separate block for each colour. To achieve multi-colour prints in a short time: with Year 5 we printed single colour blocks, then used stencilling to add a second colour; and with Year 6 we printed single blocks in a two-colour blend.

Looking after tools

Tools must be sharp. A blunt tool is hard to use and may slip while you are cutting, causing injury. Keep tools in a soft fabric roll or in a felt-lined box, or stick bottle-corks on the blades to protect them. Sharpening tools requires patience and care: use a lightly oiled carborundum or India Stone (see Bibliography for 'Handmade Prints' and other books that describe how to do it). If you are not confident sharpening tools yourself, post them to specialist suppliers who offer cheap and speedy sharpening services.

RIGHT *Victoria Park Café* by Year 5 child. Linocut print in cream-coloured ink on red Canford paper

Linocuts of the locale

Year 5 children brought pencil drawings and photos of a local London park to the lesson. They also had photos of landmarks such as Tower Bridge and the Tower of London. Each block was almost A4-sized and their sketches, on A4 paper, were to scale and so easy to copy onto blocks. My plan was to make reduction linocuts, printing each image in two or three colours. However, it took the children longer than anticipated (three hours) simply to draw and cut their images. In a further one-and-a-half-hour session, everyone completed their single colour lino-print on coloured Canford paper. This group roller-inked their own blocks and used clean rollers to print them. They learned a lot from that experience but the prints' success varied because few could exert sufficient roller-pressure to take good clear impressions. Also, the mess generated by 30 children all using inked rollers is phenomenal! It is arguable whether children learn more by printing as a group, with moderate success, or whether they learn more working one-to-one with an adult, resulting in a much higher success rate per print. I favour the latter because, after lots of effort cutting blocks, it takes only seconds to make a mess of printing them. But, on the other hand, the children had the worthwhile experience of inking and printing their blocks five or six times each.

RIGHT *Victoria Park Café* by Year 5 child. Linocut and stencil print on red Canford paper. The block was printed first in yellow ink (illustrated); then it was cleaned and re-inked in deep green. Parts of the inked block were masked out with a paper stencil before it was printed on top of the first printing, resulting in a two-colour print

British Museum, Great Court by Year 6 child. Linocut printed in yellow/black ink blend on khaki Canford paper. Photo © Madeleine Waller 2008

Later, I took this class's blocks to my studio and printed two good clear prints from each one; this ensured a good result for each child and enabled the class to see how varied printed results can be. In a later session, we made paper stencils as a quick way of printing a second colour on the lino-prints. We rolled a new colour on the lino (which had been cleaned since its last printing) and placed the stencil in position on the block, sticking it to the wet ink. The block was then laid, inked-side-down, onto the first colour print, taking care to align block edges and the image edges precisely. This block/stencil/paper 'sandwich' was then turned over, so that the paper was now on top and printed, as previously, by roller. The second colour printed only in selected areas not masked out by the stencil, resulting in a two-colour image.

RIGHT *Big Ben* by Year 6 child. Linocut print in yellow/black ink blend on blue Canford paper. Photo © Madeleine Waller 2008

Year 6 children had only one morning to make linocuts so, in advance, I cut lino blocks to half the size used for Year 5. As well as cutting with V and U gouges, some of the class created effective stippling patterns by stabbing the lino with sharp etching needles. We printed each block with a colour blend on Canford paper.

Whilst plenty of linocuts from both year groups were very good, the number of minor cutting injuries was significant and some children lacked sufficient hand-strength to get the best from the medium. There are many print techniques that can be accomplished more readily and safely by younger children – but if you like a challenge, the results children can achieve with linocutting may justify the extra effort required! Try using Softcut lino, a new, inexpensive, 'rubbery' polymer product. It cuts with V and U gouges very much more easily than lino, doesn't need sanding (it has one smooth and one textured side, both of which can be cut), and can be inked and printed in all the usual ways.

Hackney houses by Year 5 child. Linocut and stencil print in pale blue and red inks on orange Canford paper

12 Artists' books and displays of work

ARTISTS' BOOKS

Artists' books can take many forms: from handmade, handstitched, glued or stapled volumes, to miniature folded paperworks in matchboxes; from smart computer-generated publications to complex 'pop-up' paper 'sculpture' or beautifully-boxed print suites with related loose-leaf text. If planning a book, give thought to:

1 The size, shape and length of the book. These factors will set parameters as to the size, shape and weight of each artwork made for the book and the number needed to fill it.

2 Will the book be a one-off or an edition (if edition, of how many)?

3 Logistics and production costs.

4 Format – stitched, glued, concertina-folded, etc.? This will affect your choice of paper – its strength, weight and durability must be considered in relation to the format.

5 Covers – hard or soft? Involving images and/or text?

6 Text and how it relates to imagery in subject matter, layout and quantity?

7 Text production: if by hand or on computer, what fonts/style/size will be used?

8 Timescale: many books involve lengthy production time so allow sufficient time ahead of a deadline.

9 Production: will you construct it yourself or involve others?

10 Do you have the space, equipment or resources viably to produce it to your preferred format?

'Our London' books

The end goal of my project at Lauriston School was to make two large artists' books of children's prints, of a professional quality. Each contained over 70 prints from every class in the school (with related texts and poetry). One book has since been purchased by the Museum of London and the other is now in the collection of the Museum of the Guanlan Print Industry Base, Shenzhen, China.

In advance, I pre-determined that each book would involve concertina-folded pages, each page large enough to take an A4-sized print in a horizontal format (allowing a small border around each tipped-in sheet) or a slightly smaller portrait-format image. It would have hard covers made from thick mountcard covered in fabric or a printed paper (final cover decisions stayed fluid for a long time); and each double-page spread would have text on the left facing a related print on the right. I felt it should include at least five different prints per class – some 40 prints in total. In the end, I used almost twice that number per book. Whilst I pre-planned the size and shape, I had been uncertain as to the number of pages. Thus, whilst I had prepared some folded pages before the prints were selected and counted, this choice of format, as well as being straightforward to construct, could also easily be extended with extra paper sections. Once I had determined the final number of prints per book, I needed to decide how many and which prints to lay out per page and thus how many pages were needed.

The paper of both books is an inexpensive, artist's quality, 200gsm, white, Fabriano Accademia paper available in a 10x1.5m wide roll. I measured, scalpel-cut and folded the paper on a large flat worktop in my studio. Each book comprised some three, large, folded, paper sections – each join attached to the next by several neat strips of white, Filmoplast P90 (self-adhesive, archival, paper tape) at the front and back. Just as the

FACING PAGE, TOP *Our London*, one of two artists' books containing 70 children's prints in diverse techniques. The book's covers are made from thick archival mount card covered with part of a paper map of London printed (in black ink) with 12 polystyrene block prints, made by Reception Class children

FACING PAGE, BOTTOM *Our London*, detail of back cover of the same book printed (in black ink) with 13 polystyrene block prints of houses, made by Reception Class children

BELOW *Our London*, the second of two artists' books containing 70 children's prints in diverse techniques. The book's covers are made from thick archival mount card covered with a navy blue cloth, on top of which is collaged a sequence of Anne Desmet's architectural wood engravings printed in black ink on white Zerkall paper

ABOVE *Our London* book open at a page showing two of Year 3's collagraph and stencil prints (on red Lhokta paper) on the right, with related laser-printed text on the left. The book's pages are concertina folded; it can be laid on long tables and opened out to its full extent or treated as a standard book with regular page turns, as shown here

LEFT Detail of *Our London* book displayed upright along a line of tables. The section shown holds monotype (wiping method) prints by Reception Class and Year 1 children. Additional prints, not included in the books, are shown here hanging in a line from the school hall's ceiling.
Photo © Carmen Valino 2008

prints in each book were different, so too were the covers. For one set, I covered the end boards (the book's hardback covers) with a deep blue bookbinder's cloth, onto which I collaged a sequence of my own wood engraved prints on a London architectural theme. For the other book, I cut in half a large colour map of London and printed it all over, in black ink, with Reception Class's polystyrene block 'houses'. I used cornflour and water paste to glue cover cloths and printed map papers to boards, then placed all four boards, interleaved (to stop them sticking to one another) with silicone release paper (baking parchment) in a cast iron nipping press where I left them for two weeks to dry flat. (Without a press, a stack of heavy books on the boards would have done the job.) Once this was done, I pasted the first and last folded page, using cornflour paste, to the inside front and back covers of each book and pressed the books flat in the press for another 14 days.

By now the books' completion deadline was imminent so I used gluestick to attach the prints plus an A4 laser-printed page of text to each spread. The glue would dry fast without cockling so that the books would be finished without delay (with other glues, it would have been necessary to press the books for another fortnight). Having anticipated this, I had made sure that the printing papers were all of lighter weight than the book paper and not too glossy, so that the glue

Children from Lauriston school surrounding both *Our London* books, which are displayed upright along a series of tables
Photo © Carmen Valino 2008

129

would hold them firmly in place. The prints were arranged in each book in class order, from Nursery through to Year 6. Some pages featured two prints, some just one. The texts, composed by children from Reception Class upwards, extended from descriptions of their homes and gardens, to facts about London's landmarks, to inventive poetry ranging from Soho to the London Eye.

One notable problem was that some prints, while dry to touch, still offset ink onto the book's pages. To remedy this, I interleaved each page with plain paper, completely covering each 'tacky' print, and pressed the book again, for a few days, in the press. I then removed the interleaved sheets, which had picked up the excess ink. The initial offset ink on the book's pages was now completely dry and could be rubbed away with a soft eraser.

Each finished book, laid out flat, would stretch some 127 feet (c.38m) – or, roughly, the combined length of a class of 30 Year-2 children lying end to end! Neither book has ever been opened to its full extent but the beauty of concertina-folded books is that they can be opened and read, with page turns, like a regular book, or displayed propped upright in a zigzag formation, along a series of end-to-end tables.

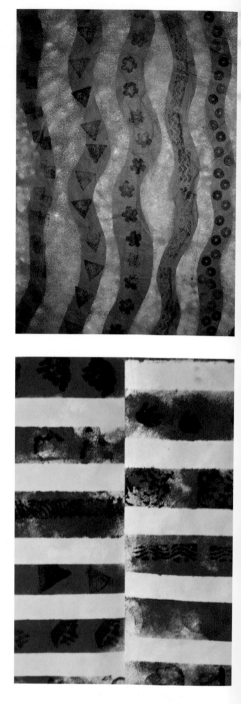

Digital books

The books were later reproduced in digital form using the iPhoto program on an AppleMac. The results were good but involved several more weeks' work and each digital book's cost was steep at around £80 (sterling) each (ordered and published online). There would certainly be cost savings, per book, if publishing in bulk rather than producing 'one-offs'.

DISPLAYING PRINTS IN SCHOOL

It is worth considering how most-effectively to display artworks on paper in a school. We're all familiar with sheets of coloured paper acting as backdrop to A4-size images but additional displays in other forms can greatly enhance the vitality and creative atmosphere of a school. Here are a few ideas:

1   Buy 30 or more picture frames, all A4 size (or A3 for more flexibility) with clip fittings for easy insertion and removal of pictures. When a picture is framed, with a nice plain wood or black moulding and white (or off-white) backing or mount card, it always looks much better than if it is simply attached, frameless, to a wall. Such frames are durable and reusable. A uniform size, colour and shape looks smart. Depending on their size, pictures can simply be slipped into an appropriate frame without needing taping to a

backing board. Children take huge pride in seeing their pictures framed. 'Ribba' frames from IKEA come in A4 or A3 sizes at less than £10 each, fit all the above specifications and look very smart.

2   If framing is not viable, think of alternative, more interesting backdrops for a display. Try sponge- or stencil-printing or even spray-painting wallpaper lining or brown paper with a pattern or tone; or (if appropriate to the display), use large sheets of patterned wallpaper, wrapping paper or fabric, or an Ordnance Survey map opened to its full extent.

3   Cover and protect displays with clear acetate (available in rolls from art materials' suppliers).

4   Clear plastic 'sleeves', all the same size, can be stapled to a board or wall and used for changing displays of art or writing.

5   Fix a 'washing line' across a room, above head height, and hang prints along its length with clothes pegs or bulldog clips.

6   Display acetate prints in windows, like stained glass.

7   Create sequential pictures (i.e., the panoramic landscapes and riverscapes: Chapters 6 and 7) that can be butted up directly against one another, to make an impressive display along a length of wall.

8   Scan or photograph a body of work and make a Powerpoint slide show for a rolling display on computer, which can be set up in a public area of the school.

Display of 'wallpapers' made by Year 1. The yellow and red striped papers fill the entire height of the wall. The horizontal stripes were created using strips of masking tape as stencils

FACING PAGE, TOP Detail of patterned paper (shown in top right of image above) made by Lauriston School staff. Paper stencil print printed with sponges (in white ink) and DIY printers (in blue/black ink) on pink Nepalese Lhokta paper

FACING PAGE, BOTTOM Detail of hand-printed wallpapers (shown in top left of image above) printed on the plain paper side of rolls of old commercially printed wallpaper. The papers were first sponge-printed in yellow ink, then masking paper strips were stuck to the wet ink (which made them easier to peel off, after printing, than had we stuck them to dry paper) and the papers sponge-printed again in red. The tape strips were peeled off and DIY printers were used to print patterns on the red stripes

Detail of red and black striped wallpaper shown on p.131. The black
details were printed using variously-textured DIY toy-brick printers

Glossary of terms, techniques and materials

Acid-free: relates to paper and archival glues and tapes. On a scale 0-14, from acidity to alkilinity, pH 7.0 is neutral.

Artists' book: book (or artwork with book traits), usually self-published by an artist or small specialist press, in a limited edition and often involving original artwork and text.

Cartridge paper: thick white paper for pencil and ink drawings.

Collage block: assemblage of card and/or other materials glued to a backing board to make a printing block.

Collagraph: print made from a collage block.

Dabber/dolly/pounce: (see pounce).

Etching needle: metal tool with sharp point used, usually, for scratching designs onto metal etching plates. It is also useful in other print processes such as lino or polystyrene printing.

Extender (**reducing medium**): transparent additive to ink that dilutes the pigment colour while maintaining the correct consistency.

Ghost print: Subsequent print(s) pulled from printing block or ink slab without first re-inking.

Hand-burnishing: printing with a hard, smooth, hand-held implement, such as a wooden or metal spoon, used to apply pressure by rubbing the back of paper laid, face down, on the inked block.

Hand/foot pressure: printing by applying pressure with hand or foot to transfer an inked impression from block to paper.

HP (hot pressed), **Not** or **CP** (cold pressed) and **Rough**: paper surfaces produced by variations in the manufacturing process.

Imprint/impression: a print.

Ink (**printing**): pigment suspended in semi-liquid oil-based or water-based medium, prepared to a particular consistency suitable for printing.

Inking slab: smooth hard surface (such as glass or marble) for mixing and rolling ink.

Japanese paper: strong, handmade paper made from the long fibres of mulberry bark and other indigenous Japanese plants; some are especially designed for printmaking.

Laid paper: imprint of light lines produced by the wires comprising the mesh base of a mould for handmade paper; it is imitated in machine-made papers.

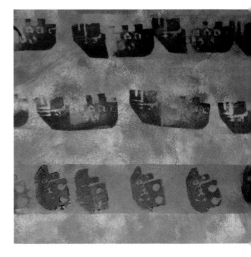

Detail of wallpaper shown on pp. 131 and 132

Limited edition: finite number of identical prints, each numbered as part of the total.

Linocut: print produced from a linoleum block.

Matrix: printing block or printing plate.

Monochrome print: print in just one colour.

Monoprint: one-off print that involves a printing matrix of some sort but which is only printed once, or has some particular added feature – e.g., hand colouring – that makes each print unique.

Monotype: one-off print, a unique impression printed from card, glass, Perspex® (Plexiglas), metal or any other surface; it cannot be repeated in identical form as it is not made from a block or other semi-permanent printing matrix.

Multiple-block printing: method using more than one block to produce an image – usually in several colours.

Offset printing: method of transferring a still-wet print from one surface to another.

Plate (printing): general term for sheet of metal, plastic, etc., from which a print is taken; largely interchangeable with block or printer but usually describes thinner printers than blocks.

Pounce/dabber/dolly: inking implement (often home-made) comprising a small piece of soft fabric or leather packed drum-tight with rags (or any soft fibre) and tied (like a tiny sack) at one end.

Printing press: machine designed to print repeatable impressions.

Printer/printing block: general term for a piece of linoleum, wood, card, etc. from which a print is taken.

Printing/printmaking: process of transferring an impression from one object onto another - rather than directly painting or drawing.

Proofs: trial impressions taken prior to editioning a final version of an image.

Reducing medium: (see extender).

Reduction method: process of making a multi-colour (or tonally graded) print from one block. The block is cut and printed in stages, each stage overprinted on top of the preceding printing. Between each printing, further cutting is carried out thereby gradually reducing the block's uncut surface. It is also known as the 'suicide method' because once it is done it cannot be undone.

Registration: alignment of multiple printings onto the same surface to ensure that each printing falls in precisely the correct position relative to the first one.

Relief print/surface print: impression produced by applying ink to the surface of a printing plate. The block's uncut surface is the area printed; cut (or indented) areas show as the paper colour.

Roller/brayer: tool used to roll out ink onto ink slab and block; can also be used for printing.

Size: dimensions of image (or paper); also gelatine or glue used to coat paper fibres internally or on the surface.

Stencil: template for design involving cut-out shapes from (usually) stiff paper, card or acetate.

U gouge: linocutting or woodcutting tool with u-shaped cutting edge (used for fairly broad cuts).

V gouge: linocutting or woodcutting tool with v-shaped cutting edge (used for fine cutting).

Waterleaf: pure, unsized paper.

Wood engraving: print produced from a block of end-grain wood using special cutting tools.

Wove paper: term for many papers which, when held up to the light, show no distinctive mark as opposed to laid papers in which a pattern of the paper mould is visible.

Toppling Skyline by Year 3 child. Collagraph (with hole-punched card), using stencilling, sponge and various DIY printers printed in red, cream and black inks on blue-green Nepalese Lhokta paper

Materials suppliers

Britain

Arboreta Papers
8 Willway Street
Bristol BS3 4BG
(Papers, especially recycled varieties and sketchbooks).

R K Burt & Co
57-61 Union Street
London SE1 1SG
www.rkburt.com (Paper).

L Cornellissen & Son Ltd
105 Great Russell Street
London WC1B 3RY
www.cornelissen.com
(Specialist printmaking supplies).

Daler-Rowney Ltd
12 Percy Street
London W1T 1DW
www.dalerrowney.co.uk
(General art supplies).

Forbo-Nairn Ltd
Kirkcaldy
Scotland
KY1 2SB
www.forbo-flooring.co.uk (Lino).

Great Art
Normandy House
1 Nether Street
Alton
Hants GU34 1EA
www.greatart.co.uk
(Mail order art and printmaking supplies).

Green & Stone of Chelsea
259 Kings Road
London SW3 5EL
www.greenandstone.com
(General art supplies).

Hawthorn Printmaker Supplies
Appleton Roebuck
York YO23 7DA
www.hawthornprintmaker.co.uk
(Rollers and oil-based, water-washable, printing inks).

IKEA
www.ikea.com
Swedish/International household furnishings store (Stockists of Ribba picture frames).

Intaglio Printmaker
62 Southwark Bridge Road
London SE1 0AS
www.intaglioprintmaker.com
(Specialist printmaking supplies including Japanese woodcutting materials and mail order).

T N Lawrence & Son Ltd
208 Portland Road
Hove
East Sussex BN3 5QT
www.lawrence.co.uk
(Specialist printmaking supplies).

Paintworks Ltd
99-101 Kingsland Road
London E2 8AG
www.paintworks.biz
(Paper, basic print supplies including Softcut lino and mail order; also specialist conservation framer of artists' prints, plus inexpensive ready-made frames).

John Purcell Papers
15 Rumsey Road
Stockwell
London SW9 OTR
www.johnpurcell.nct
(Specialist printmaking papers).

Rollaco Engineering
72 Thornfield Road
Middlesbrough
Cleveland TS5 5BY
www.rollaco.co.uk
(Specialist polyurethane printmaking rollers).

Shepherds (formerly Falkiner Fine Papers)
76 Southampton Row
London WC1B 4AR
www.bookbinding.co.uk
(Printmaking, plain and decorative papers, archival and bookbinding products).

Specialist Crafts Ltd
PO Box 247
Leicester LE1 9QS
www.specialistcrafts.co.uk
(General arts and crafts especially for children).

Yorkshire Printmakers & Distributors
26-28 Westfield Lane
Emley Moor
Nr Huddersfield, HD8 9TD
Yorkshire (Specialist printmaking supplies).

USA

American Printing Equipment & Supply Co.
Corporate HQ
153 Meacham Avenue
Elmont
NY 11003;
www.americanprintingequipment.com
(Mail order printmakers' supplies).

Baggot Leaf Co.
430 Broome Street, 2nd Floor
New York, NY 10013
www.eggtempera.com/suppliers
(Gilding supplies and metallic pigments).

Blick Art Materials
1-5 Bond Street
New York, NY 10012
www.dickblick.com/stores/newyork
(General art supplies).

Graphic Chemical and Ink Co.
732 North Yale Avenue
Villa Park
Illinois 60181
www.graphicchemical.com
(Printmaking supplies especially inks).

Kate's Paperie
72 Spring Street
New York, NY 10012; and
8 West 13th Street
New York, NY 10011
www.katespaperie.com
(Decorative papers).

Light Impressions Corp.
P.O. Box 2100
Santa Fe Springs
CA 90670
www.lightimpressionsdirect.com
(Archival storage materials, picture framing and mountboard).

Edward C Lyons
3646 White Plains Road
Bronx.
New York 10467
www.eclyons.com
(Lino tools).

New York Central Art Supply
62 3rd Avenue
New York
(Paper and printmaking supplies).

The Paper Source
2100 Central Street
Evanston
Illinois 60201
www.paper-source.com
(Decorative papers).

Pearl Paint Co.
308 Canal Street
New York
www.pearlpaint.com
(General art supplies and mail order).

Rembrandt Graphic Arts
P.O. Box 130
Rosemont
New Jersey 08556
(Printmakers' general supplies).

Sculptors' Supplies Co.
242 Elizabeth Street
New York, NY 10012
www.sculpture.org
(Wood/lino tools).

Daniel Smith Inc.
Seattle
Washington
www.danielsmith.com
(Mail order printing paper, inks, art supplies).

Takach Press Corporation
3207 Morningside NE
Albuquerque, NM 87110
www.takachpress.com
(Specialist printmaking supplies).

Utrecht Art Supply
111 Fourth Avenue between 11th and 12th
Streets
New York, NY 10003
www.utrechtart.com
(General art supplies).

Garrett Wade
5389 E. Provident Drive
Cincinnati OH 45246
www.garrettwade.com
(Wide range of wood/linocutting tools).

Zellerbach
2255 South 300 East
Salt Lake City
UT 84115
www.zellerbachonline.com (Paper).

Dragon in China Town by Year 2 child. Two-plate cereal box card print on white Somerset Satin paper. The background plate was inked in a pink/purple blend; the foreground plate was inked in red

Bibliography

Arundell, Jan & Southwell, Ray. *Design and Make Prints*. J M Dent & Sons Ltd, London 1975.

Aston, Maggy. *Printing with modelling clay*. Printmaking Today Vol. 7 No. 3 pp. 26-7. Farrand Press, London 1998.

Bodman, Sarah. *Creating Artists' Books*. A&C Black, London 2005.

D'Arcy Hughes, Ann & Vernon-Morris, Hebe. *The Printmaking Bible*. Rotovision, Hove, UK 2009.

Desmet, Anne & Anderson, Jim. *Handmade Prints – an introduction to creative printmaking without a press*. A&C Black, London; Davis, USA; & Haupt, Germany 2000; reprinted 2003 & 2006.

Digby, John & Joan. *The Collage Handbook*. Thames & Hudson, London 1985.

Duran, Catalina. *Child's Play: using modelling dough to print from 3D objects*. Printmaking Today Vol. 12 No. 3 pp 25-6. Cello Press, Oxon 2003.

Dyson, Anthony. *Printmakers' Secrets*. A&C Black, London 2009.

Erickson, Janet Doub & Sproul, Adelaide. *Print Making without a Press*. Art Horizons Inc. Reinhold, New York 1966.

Fishpool, Megan. *Hybrid Prints*. A&C Black, London 2009.

Gale, Colin. *Practical Printmaking*. A&C Black, London 2009.

Huebsch, Rand. *The Miniature Matrix: rubber stamp prints*. Printmaking Today Vol. 11 No. 3 pp 30-1. Cello Press, Oxon 2002.

Jerstorp, Karin & Kohlmark, Eva. *The Textile Design Book*. Lark Books, North Carolina USA; & A&C Black, London 1988.

Li Qingqing, Su Jianmin & Cai Lujiang. *Polystyrene prints in China's primary schools*. Printmaking Today Vol. 14 No. 3 pp. 26-7. Cello Press, Oxon 2005.

Martin, Rosie. *Strength in Diversity: 6th Form College prints*. Printmaking Today Vol. 12 No. 1 p.21. Cello Press, Oxon 2003.

Newell, Jackie & Whittington, Dee. *Monoprinting*. A&C Black, London 2006.

Robins, Deri. *Step-by-step Making Prints*. Kingfisher books, London 1993.

Samuel, Gordon & Penny, Nicola. *The Cutting Edge of Modernity. Linocuts of the Grosvenor School*. Lund Humphries, UK & USA 2002.

Simmons, Rosemary & Clemson, Katie. *The Complete Manual of Relief Printmaking*. Dorling Kindersley, London 1988.

Tala, Alexia. *Installations & Experimental Printmaking*. A&C Black, London 2009.

Tofts, Hannah. *The Print Book*. Two-Can, London 1989.

Westley, Ann. *Relief Printmaking*. A&C Black, London 2005

Print collections

Most museum print collections have a print study room where you can arrange viewings (for individuals or school groups) of a wide range of prints of your choice by booking an appointment in advance. This is a great experience, well worth doing. You can ask to see a general selection representative of the collection you are visiting, or more specific prints by particular artists.

In the UK

Ashmolean Museum, Oxford
www.ashmolean.org
(British and European prints inc. British wood engravings.)

Birmingham Museum and Art Gallery
www.bmag.org.uk/collections/print-room
(Pre-Raphaelite prints and drawings plus 1960s Kelpra Studio prints.)

British Museum, London
www.britishmuseum.org
(One of the world's greatest print collections from the 15th century to the present day.)

Fitzwilliam Museum, Cambridge
www.fitzmuseum.cam.ac.uk
(13th century to contemporary prints.)

Museum of London
www.museumoflondon.org.uk
(London-related prints; plus a Lauriston School *Our London* artists' book.)

Victoria & Albert Museum, London
www.vam.ac.uk
(Prints, posters, decorative arts.)

Whitworth Art Gallery, Manchester
www.whitworth.manchester.ac.uk
(British, European and Japanese prints plus wallpapers and textiles.)

In Europe

Albertina, Vienna
www.albertina.at

Bibliothèque Nationale, Paris
www.bnf.fr

Kupferstichkabinett, Berlin
www.berlin.de/orte/museum/kupferstichkabinett/

Rijksmuseum, Amsterdam
www.rijksmuseum.nl

Staatliche Graphische Sammlung, Munich
www.graphischesammlungen.de

In the USA

Art Institute, Chicago
www.artic.edu

Cleveland Museum of Art
www.clemusart.com

Fine Art Museum San Francisco
www.famsf.org

Fogg Art Museum, Harvard, Cambridge, Mass.
www.artmuseums.harvard.edu

LACMA: Los Angeles County Museum of Art
www.lacma.org

Metropolitan Museum of Art, New York
www.metmuseum.org

Museum of Fine Arts, Boston
www.mfa.org

National Gallery of Art, Washington
www.nga.gov

Philadelphia Museum of Art
www.philamuseum.org

Yale University Art Gallery, New Haven
artgallery.yale.edu

Index

LEFT *City skyscrapers* by Year 5 child. Linocut and stencil print in pale blue and yellow inks on black Canford paper

RIGHT *Canary Wharf skyline* by Year 4 child. Plasticine, paper stencil, sponge and DIY textured printers on Japanese Kozu-shi paper. The dark blue elements are printed from Plasticine blocks. In the taller blue tower, impressions of toy car tyre tracks and paper clips pressed into the Plasticine block can clearly be seen in the print

BELOW *Tower Bridge and the London Eye* by Year 5 child. Linocut in pale blue ink on blue Canford paper. Photo © Madeleine Waller 2008

The Author

Anne Desmet is an established artist-printmaker who specialises in wood engraving, linocut, mixed-media collage and artist's books, which she prints both with and without a press. She has taught printmaking in primary and secondary schools and has lectured in printmaking at undergraduate, postgraduate and public institutions including the Royal Academy Schools and the British Museum (both in London); she was, for four years, External Examiner for BA and MA Fine Art at Aberystwyth University. She exhibits widely, has won, over the last 20 years, some 25 awards for her prints and printed collages, has many works in public and private collections worldwide and has undertaken commissions to make prints for the British Museum, the British Library, the V&A and Sotheby's. At just 34 years old, she had a major retrospective exhibition: *Anne Desmet – Towers and Transformations* at the Ashmolean Museum, Oxford (and touring UK) in 1998-9. Ten years later, in 2008, she had a second significant museum exhibition: *Anne Desmet – Urban Evolution* at the Whitworth Art Gallery, Manchester (and touring UK) 2008-10. She is co-author, with Jim Anderson, of *Handmade Prints – an introduction to creative printmaking without a press* (A&C Black 2000; reprinted 2003 & 2006); co-editor, with Anthony Dyson, of *Printmakers: The Directory* (A&C Black 2006); and was editorial consultant to Anthony Dyson's book: *Printmakers' Secrets* (A&C Black 2009). She is also editor of *Printmaking Today* – the quarterly journal of international contemporary graphic art. She and her husband live in London with their two children.

Kite flying with St Paul's and the London Eye by Year 3 child. Polystyrene block print in a yellow/blue blend on pink Canford paper